Fourth Edition

I0209560

# CRIMINAL
# INTERROGATION

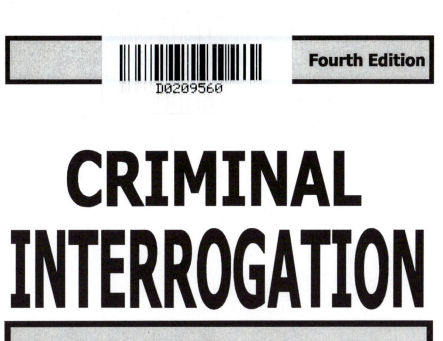

## Law and Tactics

## Devallis Rutledge, J.D.

COPPERHOUSE PUBLISHING COMPANY
P.O. Box 5463, Incline Village, Nevada 89450

**All Copperhouse titles are now distributed by**

# Atomic Dog Publishing

Atomic Dog is a higher education publishing company that specializes in developing and publishing HyBred Media™ textbooks that combine online content delivery, interactive media, and print. You can contact Atomic Dog as follows:

1148 Main Street, Third Floor
Cincinnati, OH 45202-7236
Phone: 800-310-5661     Fax: 513-842-3384
Email: copperhouse@atomicdog.com
Website: www.atomicdog.com

*Your Partner in Education*
*with*
*QUALITY BOOKS AT FAIR PRICES*

Library of Congress Catalog Number 86-71973
**ISBN 1-928916-16-3  Paper Text Edition**

3  4  5  6  7  8  9  10

*Printed in the United States of America*

# ABOUT THE AUTHOR . . .

Devallis Rutledge is also the author of *The New Police Report Manual, Courtroom Survival: The Officer's Guide to Better Testimony, The Officer Survival Manual, California Criminal Procedure* and *The Search and Seizure Handbook.*

His books are widely used by law enforcement agencies and academies, as well as colleges, throughout the nation. Rutledge is a former veteran police officer and chief assistant district attorney. Rutledge is a former member of the California Peace Officer Standards and Training (POST) Commission. He has taught law enforcement subjects to thousands through pre-service and in-service training seminars and college courses.

*Criminal Interrogation Law and Tactics*, like all his other books, is written for the field officer and student in clear, straightforward language, with scores of examples taken from real-life situations.

**ALWAYS...**
consult with your local, state, and federal authorities
for the most current information about law, policy, and procedure.

# CONTENTS

apply or was complied with? When does the 6th Amendment attach? How is it violated? What are the precautions?

A neglected area of interrogation law is explained with numerous examples and decisions. Topics include voluntariness and capacity prob-lems which frequently cause statement to be ex-cluded from trial. Proper techniques are listed.

Many interrogators fail to get all they should from a suspect who waives his rights, including the three ingredients of a criminal prosecution, con-fessions vice admissions, sealing off defense theo-ries, and more.

What a successful interrogator knows and learns about his adversary--the suspect--can make it easier to attain the objectives.

Dozens of considerations to increase the chances of obtaining a *Miranda* waiver and an admissible cop-out; four psychological ploys to eliminate the suspect's defenses; motivating factors to produce a truthful confession; tips on practicing and refining the art of interrogation.

*Chapter 14*

Factors which make all the difference between getting a cop-out, and proving it in court; technical tips for taping confessions or taking written statements; the advantages of double taping; report-writing and testifying considerations.

# TO THE READER

As someone who's been involved in police work, criminal prosecution, and law enforcement training for the past twenty-plus years, this book was exciting for me to write. I trust you'll find it revealing and rewarding to read.

No area of criminal law is more misunderstood than interrogation and confessions, and there's nothing more critical to successful enforcement than the skills of officers in getting legally admissible statements from criminals. Whether you're a municipal police officer, a county sheriff's deputy, a highway patrol officer, a federal agent or a specialized investigator, interrogation is the most highly-refined art of your profession. This is the meat of your menu.

I'm pleased that you've selected *Criminal Interrogation Law and Tactics* to help you refine your professional skills. The lawyer in me has written what I hope will be a down-to-earth summary of the legal principles you need to understand, while the cop in me added suggestions on practical tactics and techniques to help you get the admissible cop-out.

One note: most of the law affecting the admissibility of confessions comes from US Supreme Court decisions and cannot be modified by state courts or statutes; however, remember that each state can develop its own procedural rules, and these may affect you on issues which haven't yet been addressed by the Supreme Court. Be sure to consult your local supervisors, prosecutors, or criminal justice educators for information about particular procedures in your jurisdiction. For the sake of comparison (and because I'm more familiar with it), I've occasionally provided the California case law on a topic or an issue.

***Devallis Rutledge***

*Chapter 1*

# THE LOST ART
# OF INTERROGATION

Did you ever misplace something you really used —
maybe a hand tool, your favorite fishing rod, your sunglasses
or your pocket knife? Remember how sorry you were to be
without it, and how much you missed it every time you really
needed it again?

And did you ever find one of your favorite missing
items after having to do without it for awhile? Remember
how glad you were to have it back?

A lot of people in law enforcement felt in 1966 that a
favorite tool of our trade — interrogation — had been taken
away when the U.S. Supreme Court issued a decision in the
case of *Miranda v. Arizona*. (Unfortunately, a lot of people
still seem to feel that way, even though the Supreme Court
decisions of the 1980s have made dramatic efforts to preserve interrogation as a proper tool of law enforcement.)

So what has happened over the years since *Miranda* is
that the **art** of interrogation has had a serious setback. More
and more, police officers began to rely on eyewitnesses and
physical evidence, and to shy away from trying to get

admissions and confessions, so as to avoid getting involved in any complicated "*Miranda* issues."

In the first 10 years or so after *Miranda*, there seemed to be nothing but confusion about how and when an investigator could obtain a suspect's statement without navigating through a swampy maze of issues: When to warn? What is "custody?" What is "interrogation?" What about "focus?" When has the suspect invoked his rights? When has he waived? What about reopening discussions? Spontaneous statements? Inducements to talk? Improper suggestions? ... and a hundred others.

The simplest way to avoid the maze, of course, was to forget about using interrogation as a tool, and hope there was enough "external" evidence to get a conviction. Even those brave souls who tried venturing into the *Miranda* maze found themselves bumping into judges, defense attorneys, and sometimes even their local prosecutors, holding up signs saying "Wrong Way." It's difficult to find even an experienced detective who can truthfully say that he's never had a suspect's confession thrown out of court as illegally obtained.

Naturally, the more frustrating the business of interrogation became, the less often it was relied on, and the less useful confessions became in solving crimes and convicting crooks.

The impact of this post-*Miranda* decline in the use of interrogation hasn't been limited to the police profession — the entire criminal justice system has suffered, because we've been depriving ourselves of the single category of evidence that we need most — the confession. As Justice Byron White wrote in *Bruton v. U.S.*, "The defendant's own confession is probably the most probative and damaging evidence that can be admitted against him."

Think about it. Eyewitness testimony can be impeached and contradicted. A witness may have problems hearing or seeing, or remembering or describing what he or she saw. He or she may have a motive to lie or a bias that affects his or her testimony. The witness may be afraid to get involved or become a reluctant witness. Before a trial can be started, the witness may change his or her story, or forget details, or move out of the state, or even die.

And as for physical evidence, there are always questions about whether it was properly collected, properly preserved, properly analyzed, and properly introduced to prove the defendant's commission of the crime. Fingerprints can often be explained away, fibers and fluids can be refuted, and the opinions of scientific experts can be challenged.

An admissible confession, on the other hand, proves guilt all by itself. It needs no authentication, no chain of custody, no scientific examination, no opinion testimony, no inferences, and no interpretation. That's why Justice White was right — all of the physical evidence and eyewitness testimony an officer could ever compile in the investigation of any crime would not be worth as much weight *combined* as the criminal's own words, "I did it."

If the bad news is that some law enforcement officers have understandably shied away from using interrogation as their most important tool to obtain the most important kind of evidence, the good news is that it doesn't have to be that way any longer. The initial period of nervous overreaction to *Miranda* among lower court judges has generally subsided, and the Supreme Court has made it quite clear in the past several years that *Miranda* was not intended to, and need not, prevent the skillful use of interrogation in police work.

True, *Miranda* is still with us, but as you'll see in the chapters ahead, many of the "*Miranda* Myths" of the 1960s

*"Admissions of guilt are essential to society's compelling interest in finding, convicting and punishing those who violate the law."*

                                                                          *Moran v. Burbine*

and 70s have been dispelled by later court decisions. Many of the tactics and techniques which may have justifiably been thought by officers trained in the 60s and 70s to have been outlawed by *Miranda* have now been expressly approved by the Supreme Court, in a series of decisions which restore a sensible approach to the dual objectives of protecting constitutional rights and permitting effective law enforcement.

Don't believe it? Would you like some samples of some of the surprising things you're about to learn?

- There are legally permissible ways to question a suspect, after you focus suspicion on him, without giving a *Miranda* warning. (You'll find out how and why in Chapter 4.)

- There are times when it's legally permissible to use tricks and deceit to get a confession (covered in Chapter 13).

- It's sometimes permissible to re-interview a suspect without giving a new *Miranda* warning each time. Do you know when? (You'll learn in Chapter 6.)

- Even though a warning is properly given and a waiver obtained, there are other factors that may make a confession totally inadmissible. Do you know what they are? (See Chapter 2.)

- There are 4 psychological ploys that will usually remove a suspect's defenses to telling the truth and allow you to get his confession. (These and other tactics are discussed in Chapter 13.)

- Would you believe it's even possible, under certain circumstances, to question a person you suspect, in the police station, without giving any *Miranda* warning, and still obtain an admissible confession? (The cases are in Chapter 4.)

Mastering the skill of lawful interrogation isn't, as some officers dreadfully fear, a tedious task of memorizing an endless set of rules to get you through the swampy maze. It's simple, and it's fairly easy, once you go *behind* the rules and get a basic understanding of where the rules came from and why they came about.

Instead of trying to memorize rules, let's just analyze a few basic concepts about why people make incriminating statements to police. Get these basics down, and the court decisions will begin to fit together, the need to carry a rule book will disappear, and the confidence in the interrogation process will resume. The swampy maze will dry up.

The art of interrogation hasn't been permanently lost to law enforcement officers — it's just been misplaced for awhile. If you're ready to oil it up and make full use of it again, let's get started.

(Incidentally, "interrogation" does not mean "interview." Please don't be offended by the use of the word "interrogation"; let's agree — for purposes of this book — that as contrasted to the less-structured process of "interviewing," an interrogation is **controlled questioning** calculated to discover and confirm the truth from the responses of an individual, in spite of his intentions and efforts to conceal it.)

*Chapter 2*

# INTERROGATION AND THE 4TH AMENDMENT

## Searching, Seizing, and Questioning

It's understandable that when most people think of interrogation, they think only of *Miranda*. There's no question that the *Miranda* issues are the most common issues litigated in deciding the admissibility of a suspect's statement.

However, *Miranda* is neither the first nor the last word in confession admissibility. Actually, before a judge will allow a confession into evidence, he puts it through a *four-part* Constitutional test, only one part of which has anything to do with *Miranda* compliance.

If the judge is going to use a four-part test, the prosecutor has to use it in evaluating your cases for charging and trial. And if the prosecutor is going to use the four-part test, you have to use it, too, or your cases won't get prosecuted if they depend on the admissibility of the confession you obtained to get a conviction.

What are the four parts? They are the 4th, 5th, 6th and 14th Amendment tests. A confession (or any statement by the accused, whether exculpatory or inculpatory) is inadmissible if it was obtained in violation of any *one* of these four Constitutional provisions. Put another way, the confession has to pass all four of these tests (not just *Miranda*) to be admissible in evidence.

The *Miranda* decision relates to the 5th Amendment right against compelled self-incrimination (see discussion in Chapter 3). Other significant Supreme Court decisions have held confessions inadmissible under the 4th Amendment (as resulting from illegal seizures, discussed here), under the 6th Amendment (as violating the right to counsel, discussed in Chapter 9), and under the 14th Amendment (as violating the "due process" clause, see Chapter 10).

**You can't be a skilled, effective interrogator without understanding the effects of these four amendments on the admissibility of confession evidence.** You might still be able to get a cop-out, but that's not the same as getting it admitted into evidence in court.

So let's simply take them in order, beginning with the Fourth Amendment:

> The right of the people to be secure in their persons, houses, papers, and effects, against unreasonable searches and seizures, shall not be violated, and no warrant shall issue, but upon probable cause, supported by Oath or affirmation, and particularly describing the place to be searched, and the persons or things to be seized.

The cases applying the Fourth Amendment to the admissibility of confessions define two separate issues:

(1)  did the method of overhearing the suspect's statements amount to an illegal *search*, or

(2)  was a confession obtained as a direct result of an illegal *seizure* (arrest)?

In everyday police work, the first of these situations is pretty rare. An example of a situation where the problem occurred is in *Katz v. US*, where officers illegally bugged a public phone booth and recorded the crook's conversation with his confederate. Since a citizen can reasonably expect privacy in a closed telephone booth, the warrantless bugging amounted to an illegal *search*, according to the Supreme Court. The overheard incriminating statements, therefore, were inadmissible.

On the other hand, if the crook carelessly makes incriminating statements at open phone stations, where nearby eavesdroppers might overhear, there is no Fourth Amendment problem in your standing around in a public place and overhearing:

> The risk of being overheard by an eavesdropper or betrayed by an informer or deceived as to the identity of one with whom one deals is probably inherent in the conditions of human society. It is the kind of risk we necessarily assume whenever we speak.
>
> *Lopez v. US*, at 470

Also, there's no forbidden search if you go undercover — or send in a wired informant — to transmit or record or memorize an *unindicted* (uncharged) suspect's out-of-custody statements. The Fourth Amendment does not protect "a wrongdoer's misplaced belief that a person to whom he voluntarily confides his wrongdoing will not reveal it." *Hoffa v. US; US v. White.*

As to the second kind of Fourth Amendment issue involving statements — whether they resulted from an illegal seizure — this kind of problem is, unfortunately, much more common in everyday police work. If the court determines that you illegally detained or arrested (seized) a suspect, his resulting confession will probably be inadmissible, *in spite of your compliance with Miranda.*

For example, in *Brown v. Illinois*, a murder suspect was illegally arrested, without probable cause. After receiving a *Miranda* warning and waiving his rights, he made incriminating statements. The Supreme Court noted that under the holding of *Wong Sun v. US* (the so-called "fruit of the poisonous tree" case), a suspect's confession after an illegal arrest could only be admissible if there had been some intervening act to "attenuate the taint" and show that the suspect's confession was an act of *free will.*

The prosecutor in *Brown v. Illinois* argued that the suspect's waiver of his *Miranda* rights should be enough to attenuate the taint of his illegal arrest. But the Supreme Court disagreed:

> ...the Miranda warnings, alone and per se, cannot always make the act sufficiently a product of free will to break, for Fourth Amendment purposes, the causal connection between the illegality and the confession.
> *Brown v. Illinois*, at 603

Instead of merely looking for a *Miranda* waiver after an illegal arrest, the Supreme Court held that it would be necessary to consider five factors before deciding whether to admit a confession in court:

(1)  *Miranda* waiver;

(2)  how much time has passed between the illegal arrest and the confession (the longer, the better);

(3)  how serious and deliberate the officers' misconduct was in making an illegal arrest;

(4)  any intervening circumstances; and

(5)  the voluntariness of the statement (see Chapter 10).

When the Supreme Court looked at these five factors in Brown's case, they held that his statements were inadmissible, on the basis of the other 4 factors, even though there had been a *Miranda* waiver.

Two similar cases, where confessions were not held admissible despite *Miranda* waivers after illegal arrests, were *Dunaway v. New York* and *Taylor v. Alabama*. Both of these cases (one a murder, the other a robbery) passed the *Miranda* test, but failed on the other factors, because of no intervening circumstances, only a short interval of time (2-6 hours), and flagrant police misconduct in making arrests without probable cause, "in the hope that something would turn up."

So as you can see, a *Miranda* waiver won't necessarily cure an illegal arrest. You can't rely on your skill at getting suspects to waive their rights and to confess in order to solve a difficult case if you've arrested your suspect without probable cause.

*"The defendant's own confession is probably the most probative and damaging evidence that can be admitted against him."*

*Bruton v. US*

Do any cases ever go the other way? Yes. After considering all five factors in the case of *Rawlings v. Kentucky*, the Supreme Court held the suspect's statements admissible — he waived *Miranda*; his statements were voluntary; there were intervening circumstances (suspect made spontaneous statements on seeing the police find drugs in a search of the house, under warrant); there was only a 45-minute interim between illegal detention and the statements, but the police misconduct was not flagrant or deliberate (they thought they could detain Rawlings because of the warrant), and it was not as serious as *Brown, Dunaway* and *Taylor* (Rawlings was only illegally *detained* at the time of his statement — not illegally *arrested*).

*Wong Sun v. US* is another case. Although Wong Sun had been illegally arrested, he had been released (intervening event) and voluntarily returned to the station the next day (free will) to make incriminating statements, so the Court held these admissible.

Obviously, the safest way for you to avoid Fourth Amendment problems in obtaining statements from suspects is to know and follow the laws of search and seizure. Any time you're uncertain of your grounds for detaining or arresting someone, it would be better either to get a warrant, or to try to get the statement in a *non-custodial* setting, so that neither *Miranda* nor the 4th Amendment would apply (see Chapter 4).

*Chapter 3*

# INTERROGATION AND THE 5TH AMENDMENT

## Compelling Incrimination

The *Miranda* decision is 63 pages long — not counting concurring and dissenting opinions. It's perfectly understandable that most law enforcement officers haven't read the opinion. (If a survey were taken, it would probably find that many judges and criminal attorneys haven't read it, either.)

But if you've never read it, you've probably never really understood it. Unless you've read it, you may not realize *why* you have to read that "*Miranda* card" to a suspect before beginning custodial interrogation. And if you don't have a good, clear understanding of the *why*, you won't be able to figure out for yourself *when* you have to *Mirandize*, and when you don't. You'll be stuck trying to memorize a million rules. The better, easier thing is to simply look inside *Miranda* and get a handle on the *why*.

You're not going to have to read all 63 pages of *Miranda* to get to the bottom of things — the important parts are covered here in this book. But you are going to need to read these words, extracted from the Fifth Amendment, because they are the *source* of all of the *Miranda* rules:

> No person...shall be compelled in any Criminal Case to be a witness against himself....

What is the secret word? **"Compelled."**

There were times, throughout history, when people accused of crimes could be summoned into the king's court and made to answer incriminating questions. But this inquisitorial system of justice was too easily and too often abused for personal or political purposes, with the result that innocent, falsely-accused people suffered.

So when the authors of the US Constitution realized that a bill of individual rights was needed, they included the provision above, that prohibits the government from compelling an accused criminal to be a witness against himself.

That doesn't simply mean that the government cannot call the defendant to the witness stand. It means that the government cannot compel the defendant to make *any* statements, at *any* stage of an investigation or court proceedings.

What does this have to do with *Miranda*? After all, Ernesto Miranda hadn't been tortured into talking to Phoenix police about the kidnap-rape case he was arrested on. He had merely been interrogated for a couple of hours, and then signed a confession. So where was the *compulsion*?

It was *inherent*, said the Supreme Court, in the process of interrogation while in police custody. The majority of justices deciding the *Miranda* case reasoned that the prospect of being questioned by police while in their custody would be so frightening to the individual citizen that it would compel him to say things he might not otherwise have said. In other words, not only would the government be compelling an accused to be a witness against himself by calling him to testify at his trial, it would also be compelling self-incrimination during the investigation by subjecting him to questioning that was inherently coercive:

> The current practice of incommunicado interrogation is at odds with one of our Nation's most cherished principles — that the individual may not be compelled to incriminate himself.
>
> *Miranda*, at 457

> Custodial arrest is said to convey to the suspect a message that he has no choice but to submit to the officers' will and to confess. It thrusts an individual into an interrogation environment created for no purpose other than to subjugate the individual to the will of his examiner.
>
> *Minnesota v. Murphy*, at 423

In coming to this conclusion, the Supreme Court looked at standard interrogation practices, such as isolating the suspect from familiar surroundings, questioning him continuously for hours and hours with "tag teams" of rested interrogators, using the "Mutt and Jeff" routine (one "friendly" interrogator saving the defenseless suspect from a "hostile" interrogator, and thereby gaining his confidence and getting him to talk), and telling the suspect how bad it will look for him if he doesn't give any explanation for the crime he's accused of.

These and similar interrogation techniques, said the court, amounted to a form of compulsion that made it difficult for the suspect to maintain his presence of mind so that he could exercise his right to remain silent:

> It is important to keep the subject off balance, for example, by trading on his insecurity about himself or his surroundings. The police then persuade, trick or cajole him out of exercising his constitutional rights.

> ...the very fact of custodial interrogation exacts a heavy toll on individual liberty and trades on the weakness of individuals....In other settings, these individuals might have exercised their constitutional rights. In the incommunicado police-dominated atmosphere, they succumbed.

> An individual swept from familiar surroundings into police custody, surrounded by antagonistic forces, and subjected to the techniques of persuasion described above cannot be otherwise than under compulsion to speak.
> *Miranda*, at 455,461

Once the Supreme Court had come to the conclusion that custodial interrogation was *necessarily* compulsive, and therefore contrary to the Fifth Amendment, what could be done? Knowing how vital interrogation and confessions were to effective criminal justice, the Supreme Court members were not willing to outlaw custodial interrogation altogether. But they did feel it was necessary to do something to *neutralize* the coercive atmosphere of police questioning, so that individual citizens could decide — free from intimidation — whether or not to talk to police.

What would it take to neutralize the inherent compulsion? The Court gave *two* acceptable alternatives, either one of which it considered sufficiently protective to neutralize custodial coercion: (1) the presence of an attorney, or (2) the advice of rights now commonly called the "*Miranda* warning."

The *Miranda* decision was one of four decisions issued together on June 13, 1966, concerning the admissibility of statements obtained through custodial interrogation. Said the Court, in acknowledging that an attorney would have sufficed to neutralize inherent compulsion:

> The presence of counsel, in all the cases before us today, would be the adequate protective device necessary to make the process of police interrogation conform to the dictates of the privilege. His presence would insure that statements made in the government-established atmosphere are not the product of compulsion.
>
> *Miranda*, at 466

This means that if you should ever have a situation where the suspect in custody has his attorney present when you begin interrogation, no *Miranda* warning or waiver is required. (This would probably be very rare, except perhaps for a case where the attorney is convinced that his client is innocent and that discussions with you will result in his release.)

The second neutralizing device—the familiar *Miranda* warning—was the Court's only other pre-approved method of insuring that custodial statements were not compelled (the Court left open the possibility that *other* means of protecting the Fifth Amendment privilege might later be approved—see page 467 of the decision—but, to date, none has been, and in *Dickerson v. U.S.*, the Court ruled that a federal statute enacted by Congress was not sufficient to replace the warning).

And now you know the Supreme Court's rationale for requiring you to read (or recite) the suspect's rights to him before beginning custodial interrogation:

> We have concluded that without proper safeguards the process of in-custody interrogation of persons suspected or accused of crime contains inherently compelling pressures which work to undermine the individual's will to resist and to compel him to speak where he would not otherwise do so freely. In order to combat these pressures and to permit a full opportunity to exercise the privilege against self-incrimination, the accused must be adequately and effectively apprised of his rights and the exercise of those rights must be fully honored.
>
> *Miranda*, at 467

> Other US Supreme Court decisions since *Miranda* have repeated the purpose of the warnings: The function of the warnings relates to the Fifth Amendment's guarantee against coerced self-incrimination....
>
> *Brown v. Illinois*, at 600

> All *Miranda*'s safeguards, which are designed to avoid the coercive atmosphere, rest on the overbearing compulsion which the Court thought was caused by isolation of a suspect in police custody.
>
> *US v. Washington*, Fn.5

Since we now know that the *Miranda* warnings are required, in the absence of an attorney, to counter-balance the inherently compelling atmosphere of custodial interrogation, we now know — without memorizing any rules — when it is *not* necessary to give the warnings: when there's nothing to counter-balance:

> To dissipate the overbearing compulsion caused by isolation of a suspect in custody, the *Miranda* court required the exclusion of incriminating statements obtained during custodial interrogation unless the suspect fails to claim the Fifth Amendment privilege after being suitably warned of his right to remain silent and of the consequences of his failure to assert it. We have consistently held, however, that his extraordinary safeguard does not apply outside the context of the inherently coercive custodial interrogations for which it was designed.
>
> *Minnesota v. Murphy*, at 421

When are *Miranda* warnings required? Before you begin custodial interrogation. When are they *not* required? When your interrogation is of a suspect who is not in *custody*, or when a suspect in custody makes statements which are

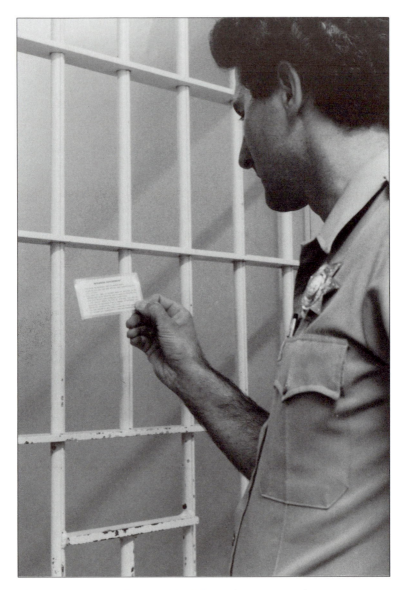

*Illegal custody isn't cured by Miranda waivers alone.*

not the product of *interrogation*. The two-part test for determining whether or not you have to *Mirandize* someone, therefore, is simply:

(1) Is he in custody?

(2) Is he being interrogated?

If the answer to either question is "**No**," *Miranda* does not apply, for without custodial interrogation there is no inherently compelling situation which requires the neutralizing device of warnings.

However, to answer these two questions for yourself in any particular circumstances you may confront in your cases, you need to know what is and isn't "custody" and "interrogation," for *Miranda* purposes. Read on.

*Chapter 4*

# CUSTODY

Some people in law enforcement think there's a very easy way to resolve any confusion about *Miranda* — they simply read the warning to *everyone*, before *every* interview or attempted interrogation.

What's wrong with that? What's wrong is that they're overlooking the meaning of the word "warning" in the phrase, "*Miranda* warning."

A "warning" is a notice of danger. It's a means of making someone aware of the need for caution. It's intended to arouse the defenses of the person being warned. A warning is a red flag.

When you need to get information about how a crime occurred by asking questions of someone who may have been involved, your job will be made easier if the person you need to question will willingly and readily give you answers. Obviously, a person will be less willing to talk to you if you start the interview by waving a red flag and telling the person that he may be endangering himself by answering your questions.

Indeed, as we saw in the last chapter, the *Miranda* warning was specifically designed by the Supreme Court as a notice of danger to suspects being subjected to custodial interrogation. It was meant to be a red flag to be waved by the interrogator to caution the suspect about the dangers of proceeding, and to remind him that he could keep his mouth shut and ask for a lawyer.

Let's compare the interrogation process to a highway trip for the suspect. He starts off down the road and reaches a cruising speed of 55 miles per hour. Then up ahead he sees a flagman, waving a red flag. Then he sees a bright orange sign that says, "Danger. Highway Construction. Rough Road. 25 MPH." What does the suspect do?

If you've ever worked traffic, you know that perhaps 3 out of 10 motorists who see the flagman and the sign will completely disregard the warnings and cruise on at 55 MPH. Maybe 4 others will reduce their speed somewhat and become more alert. And the other 3 motorists will slow down to the cautionary speed of 25 MPH.

The point is that while a few people traveling the suspect's route may completely disregard the warnings and cruise right on into "danger," most people will respond to the warnings in one way or another, and a few will do exactly what the warnings caution them to do.

It's the same with *Miranda*. As you know, some people who are foolish enough to commit crimes are foolish enough to admit it. Some suspects are going to disregard the *Miranda* warnings you give and cop their fool heads out, full speed ahead. Others, however, are going to engage certain defenses against telling you the truth, while the remaining percentage of suspects are going to do exactly what the warnings caution them to do — they're going to dummy up and demand a lawyer.

Knowing that the *Miranda* warning will often accomplish precisely what the Supreme Court designed it to accomplish, and knowing that this will invariably make your job more difficult, why would you ever want to start waving the red flag when you don't need to? Giving a warning when it isn't legally required is like putting out danger signs when there's absolutely nothing wrong with the road. It's an unnecessary obstacle.

It's fairly common for prosecuting attorneys to advise police officers *always* to *Mirandize*. That's because it makes the prosecutor's job easier in court. What some prosecutors may be forgetting, however, is that they would never even *see* some cases if you went around needlessly trying to talk suspects out of answering your questions. If you aren't able to *solve* a case, the prosecutor isn't going to be able to *prosecute* it.

So it won't do for you to simply *Mirandize* everyone you want to talk to. To return to our highway analogy, that would be like keeping the signs out permanently, just to be sure that motorists were cautioned on those few days when the road really was dangerous. You would unnecessarily slow down the natural flow of traffic, just to be safe on the few occasions when caution was actually needed.

The better practice is to be able to tell when the red flag is needed, and when it isn't, and never to merely pull it out and start waving it automatically. The red flag we call the "*Miranda* warning" only has to be waved before you begin to engage in custodial interrogation. Therefore, instead of taking the approach that you should always *Mirandize*, "just to be safe," you would be better advised never to *Mirandize*, unless you have a "custodial interrogation" situation. Otherwise, you're needlessly shutting people up in a great many cases when you need their answers to solve crimes and to give the prosecutor something to prosecute.

When do you have "custodial interrogation," and when don't you?

> By custodial interrogation, we mean ques-
> tioning initiated by law enforcement officers
> after a person has been taken into custody or
> otherwise deprived of his freedom of action
> in any significant way.
>
> *Miranda*, at 444

In Chapter 5, we'll get to the question of when you're engaged in "questioning" and when you aren't. But first, let's look at the issue of "custody."

A suspect is obviously in custody if he's in prison, in jail, or in any other kind of police lock-up facility. Therefore, you have to *Mirandize* before questioning in any of these settings, even if you're undercover, and even if the suspect is in jail in another jurisdiction, for an unrelated offense. (*Mathis v. US*)

A suspect is also in custody if he's locked in a police car, or has been handcuffed, or has been told he's under arrest. It has even been ruled, in *Orozco v. Texas*, that a suspect was in custody in the bedroom of his own home, where he was surrounded by four armed police officers who said that he was "under arrest."

On the other hand, "transitory restraints" on a person's liberty, such as during a traffic stop or a field interview, would not ordinarily be considered as depriving an individual of his freedom of action in any significant way:

> General on-the-scene questioning as to
> facts surrounding a crime or other general
> questioning of citizens in the fact-finding

process is not affected by our holding. It is an act of responsible citizenship for individuals to give whatever information they may have to aid in law enforcement. In such situations, the compelling atmosphere inherent in the process of in-custody interrogation is not necessarily present.

*Miranda*, at 477


*Miranda*, of course, did not reach investigative questioning of a person not in custody...and it assuredly did not indicate that such questioning ought to be deemed inherently coercive.

*Schneckloth v. Bustamonte*


...the ultimate inquiry is whether there is a formal arrest or restraint on freedom of movement of the degree associated with a formal arrest.

*California v. Beheler*

In any contact or detention where there is less restriction on a person than that degree associated with a formal arrest, no warning need be given, because there is no "custody." That's why it isn't necessary to *Mirandize* someone you stop for a traffic citation, nor to *Mirandize* the DUI motorist at your initial contact; the Supreme Court has ruled that before a DUI suspect has been taken into custody, he may be subjected to a field balance test and may be asked "a modest number of questions" about his drinking and driving. (*Berkemer v. McCarty*)

The absence of custody is what allows you to *telephone* a suspect and ask him all the incriminating questions you want to, without a *Miranda* warning (obviously, to make use of his answers, you would have to have some way to prove it was the suspect on the other end of the line). When a person is talking to the police by telephone, from his own home or workplace, for example, he is not being subjected to any inherently compelling circumstances — he could simply hang up the phone, if he wanted to.

It's the absence of custody that allows the IRS to make use of incriminating answers to questions on tax forms. A taxpayer's freedom of movement isn't restricted when he fills out a tax return in the privacy of his own home, or at his accountant's office (*Garner v. US*). Likewise, if your department has a written form that you send to suspects to answer and return (in NSF check cases or traffic accident cases, for example), *Miranda* does not apply — there's no custody connected to your interrogation.

And it's the absence of custody that allows you to ask questions without *Mirandizing,* even though your suspicions have focused on the suspect you're dealing with, so long as you haven't significantly restricted his freedom of movement. Here's where we dispel another *Miranda* myth.

In *Escobedo v. Illinois,* which was decided by the Supreme Court 2 years before *Miranda,* the Court used the word "focus" in discussing the point at which the suspect's right to an attorney arose. Unfortunately, many people in law enforcement grafted the concept of focus onto *Miranda,* and perpetuated the myth that it was necessary for an officer to *Mirandize* a person whenever the officer's suspicions focused on that suspect.

Once this myth had been conjured up, defense attorneys began asking police officers on the witness stand about the officers' subjective states of mind, as though the thoughts inside an officer's head could somehow constitute custody. The standard defense question on focus was, "Officer, in your mind, was the suspect free to go at that point?" When the officer said, "No," defense attorneys and some judges and prosecutors took the position that custody occurred, and that *Miranda* applied.

Whatever may have been going through an officer's mind during his encounter with a suspect is irrelevant, however, because the Supreme Court and state courts have declared that the subjective "focus" of an officer's suspicions is *not* tantamount to an arrest:

> [...questioning initiated by law enforcement officers after a person has been taken into custody or otherwise deprived of his freedom of action in any significant way]...is what we meant in *Escobedo* when we spoke of an investigation which had focused on an accused.
>
> *Miranda*, Fn.4

> ...the major thrust of [defendant's] argument is that the principle of *Miranda* should be extended to cover interrogation in noncustodial circumstances after a police investigation has focused on the suspect. We are not impressed with this argument....

> *Miranda* specifically defined "focus," for its purposes, as questioning initiated by officers after a person has been taken into custody

or otherwise deprived of his freedom of action in any significant way.

*Beckwith v. US*

Police officers are not required to render *Miranda* warnings to everyone whom they question. Nor is the requirement of warnings to be imposed simply because the questioned person is one whom the police suspect.

*Oregon v. Mathiason*

Our holding in *Mathiason* reflected our earlier decision in *Beckwith v. US* in which we rejected the notion that the "in custody" requirement was satisfied merely because the police interviewed a person who was the "focus" of a criminal investigation.

*California v. Beheler*, Fn.2

A police officer's unarticulated plan has no bearing on the question whether the suspect was "in custody" at a particular time.

*Berkemer v. McCarthy*

A police officer's subjective focus of suspicion "does not bear upon the question whether the individual is in custody for purposes of Miranda."

*Stansbury v. California*

Seen enough? The applicability of *Miranda* to the facts of any particular case has nothing whatsoever to do with whether or not you had focused suspicion on the suspect, or whether in your mind he was free to leave. The test is simply whether a reasonable person in the suspect's position would have felt that he was under arrest, or was being restricted to the degree associated with arrest. *Hocus focus.*

It's easy to demonstrate that focus doesn't invoke *Miranda.* Suppose you get all kinds of reliable information (fingerprints and eyewitnesses, for example) pointing to the guilt of an auto thief you've arrested several times before. Your suspicion will be focused on this individual, won't it? But if you decide to telephone him and ask him some incriminating questions, will you have to *Mirandize*? Of course not — he's not in custody. There's an illustration of the proof that focus is not a factor in determining when to Mirandize. (Others include questioning at his home or job, when he hasn't been taken into custody.)

Now that you know two facts (that the purpose of *Miranda* is to neutralize the inherent compulsion of custodial interrogation, and that your subjective focus on the suspect is irrelevant to *Miranda*), it should be clear to you that it's possible to question someone you suspect of a crime any-place, anytime, without giving a *Miranda* warning, provided the suspect is not in custody.

In the *Beckwith* case, for example, IRS investigators went to the suspect's home to question him about criminal tax fraud they suspected him of having committed. Beckwith talked with the officers at his dining table for approximately 3 hours, without a *Miranda* waiver. Before his trial, Beckwith tried to suppress his incriminating statements on the ground that he had not been given a *Miranda* warning after suspicion had focused on him. Holding that Beckwith had not been "in custody" during the questioning and that "focus" was irrel-evant, the Supreme Court ruled his statements admissible.

Another example of non-custodial questioning where *Miranda* was held not to apply was in *Minnesota v. Murphy.* Murphy was on probation for a sex crime when he went to his probation officer's office for an interview. During this interview, and without any *Miranda* warning, Murphy incriminated himself in a murder case. He was later convicted of the murder and appealed to the Supreme Court to rule that he should have been *Mirandized* once suspicion focused on him. The Supreme Court refused, and affirmed his conviction:

> The mere fact that an investigation has focused on a suspect does not trigger the need for *Miranda* warnings in noncustodial settings, and the probation officer's knowledge and intent have no bearing on the outcome of this case.
>
> *Minnesota v. Murphy*

A more extreme example of non-custodial interrogation without *Miranda* is *Oregon v. Mathiason,* where a burglary suspect was asked to meet a police officer at a nearby state patrol office for questioning. The officer took the suspect into a room, told him he was not under arrest, closed the door, and told him he was suspected of the burglary. Mathiason then gave incriminating answers.

After getting admissions from Mathiason, the officer then read him his *Miranda* rights, took a waiver, tape recorded a full confession and then released Mathiason. The officer told him the case would be submitted to the district attorney for a decision.

When the DA filed charges and introduced Mathiason's statements, Mathiason complained, pointing out that he had been questioned in a police station, and arguing that this was indicative of custody. The Oregon court agreed, but the US Supreme Court, noting that the officer had not restricted Mathiason's freedom of movement and had specifically told him he was *not* under arrest, said,

> Such a noncustodial setting is not converted to one in which Miranda applies simply because a reviewing court concludes that, even in the absence of any formal arrest or restraint on freedom of movement, the questioning took place in a "coercive environment."

> Nor is the requirement of warnings to be imposed simply because the questioning takes place in the station house....
>
> *Oregon v. Mathiason*

Similarly, in *California v. Beheler*, a murder suspect went into the police station voluntarily, on the officer's assurances that he was not under arrest. He was questioned for 30 minutes, without *Miranda*, and then released, being told the district attorney would be evaluating the case.

Beheler was subsequently convicted of first-degree murder, partly on the basis of his statements to police. When he appealed to the California Court of Appeal, that court held that he should have been Mirandized, since he was questioned at the police station after suspicion had focused on him. But the US Supreme Court disagreed with California's ruling and held that *Miranda* did not apply:

*Custodial interrogation is deemed by the courts to be "inherently compelling."*

> We have explicitly recognized that *Miranda*
> warnings are not required simply because the
> questioning takes place in the station house,
> or because the questioned person is one whom
> the police suspect.
>
> *California v. Beheler*

So as you can see, it isn't the *place* where questioning takes place that determines whether or not you have to *Mirandize*, and it isn't the *focus* of your suspicions. It is, instead, the degree to which you have restricted the suspect's freedom of movement as of the time questioning begins.

Tactical considerations on when and how to *Mirandize* in view of the definition of "custody" are covered in Chapter 13.

But custody is only half of the test for *Miranda* — the other half requires that you understand the court's definition of "interrogation." We take that up next, in Chapter 5.

## Chapter 5

# INTERROGATION AND ITS FUNCTIONAL EQUIVALENT

If you were to read the *Miranda* decision, you would notice that it did not say that a police officer had to give a warning before *listening* to a suspect's statements. Rather, the warning is required before an officer begins *interrogation* of a suspect who's in custody. This simple fact explains why we have the so-called "spontaneous declaration" category of statements — things the suspect said on his own, without any police prompting.

Remember, if you aren't firing questions at the suspect, he isn't being subjected to any inherently compelling pressures, and therefore there's no need for the counter-balance of the red-flag warning. The suspect is simply exercising his free will:

> In dealing with statements obtained through interrogation, we do not purport to find all confessions inadmissible. Confessions remain a proper element in law enforcement. Any statement given freely and voluntarily with-

out any compelling influences is, of course, admissible in evidence.

The fundamental import of the privilege while an individual is in custody is not whether he is allowed to talk to the police without the benefit of warnings and counsel, but whether he can be interrogated.

There is no requirement that police stop a person who enters a police station and states that he wishes to confess to a crime, or a person who calls the police to offer a confession or any other statement he desires to make.

Volunteered statements of any kind are not barred by the Fifth Amendment and their admissibility is not affected by our holding today.

*Miranda*, at 478

Therefore, if a suspect in custody starts telling you something, do *not* interrupt him with your red flag. No *Miranda* warning is required as long as you're simply listening, and not asking questions or making comments to draw out more details. You can listen to a suspect's volunteered confessions all day long, write them down verbatim, or tape record them, without *Miranda* ever crossing your mind or your lips.

It's the absence of interrogation that allows you to place two or more suspects together in the back of your police car, turn on a concealed tape recorder, and leave them alone to "get their stories straight;" for *Miranda* purposes, no advisement is necessary, and their statements are admissible, because they're not the product of custodial *interrogation*.

However, you need to be aware that it's not only express questioning that's considered to be interrogation — it's also the "functional equivalent" of questioning. For example, in *Brewer v. Williams*, police captured a murder suspect in one city and were driving him back to the city where the crime occurred. Williams had cut off questioning by telling the officers he wanted to talk to his attorney.

The murder victim in the Williams case was a young girl, and as the police car drove through snow-covered countryside, one of the officers turned to Williams and told him that "the parents of this little girl should be entitled to a Christian burial." The officer pointed out that with the coming snowfall, the girl's body, wherever it had been dumped, might be covered over and never found.

This "Christian burial speech" prompted Williams to relent and show the officers where he had dumped the girl's body. His statements telling where the body could be found were offered against him at trial, but the Supreme Court ruled Williams' invocation of his right to consult his attorney had not been honored by the officers, and the statements could not be used against him.

Notice that the "Christian burial speech" did not amount to express questioning. The officer did not "ask a question" of Williams in the traditional sense. But the Supreme Court found that the officer's use of the story about the little girl's parents was designed to provoke the suspect into giving information, which is the same purpose a question serves:

> There can be no serious doubt that [the officer] deliberately and designedly set out to

> elicit information from Williams just as surely
> as — and perhaps more effectively than — if
> he had formally interrogated him.
>
> *Brewer v. Williams*

In a somewhat similar case but with a critical distinction that produced a different result, police officers in Rhode Island arrested a man suspected of murdering a taxicab driver with a sawed-off shotgun. The suspect didn't have the gun on him at the time of his arrest near a school for handicapped children.

Enroute to the police station with their prisoner, the 2 officers talked *to each other* (but not directly to the suspect) about the dangers of the handicapped children finding the shotgun and getting hurt. Overhearing these comments, the suspect volunteered the location of the gun. His statements were introduced at trial, and the suspect was convicted of murder.

The Supreme Court, noting that the comments between officers in this case were *not* specifically aimed at the suspect or designed to provoke him into talking, held that no interrogation had occurred, and the statements were therefore admissible.

In so doing, the Supreme Court made clear that *Miranda* does apply not only to questioning, but also to any act by police intended to provoke an incriminating response:

> ...the *Miranda* safeguards come into play
> whenever a person in custody is subjected to
> either express questioning or its functional
> equivalent.
>
> *Rhode Island v. Innis*

*A suspect can lawfully be interrogated without Miranda —
even in the police station — as long as it is made clear that he
is not in custody.*

And just exactly what is the "functional equivalent" of questioning?

> ...any words or actions on the part of the police (other than those normally attendant to arrest and custody) that the police should know are reasonably likely to elicit an incriminating response from the suspect.
>
> *Innis*, at 300

This means you don't have to *Mirandize* before asking normal booking questions, such as name, address, physical description, date of birth, and general medical condition. You can't overdo it, however, and put investigative questions on your booking slip.

It also means that if you say or do anything to the suspect that you should know is reasonably likely to produce an incriminating response, and provided your suspect is in custody, *Miranda* applies, and warnings are required.

And now, knowing what you know about custodial interrogation, you should be able to figure out when you have to *Mirandize*, and when you don't, by simply asking yourself, "Is the suspect in custody?" and "Am I engaged in interrogation?"

For example, you answer a disturbance call and find a crowd around a wounded victim. You ask, "What happened here?" and a man standing over the victim says, "He insulted my old lady, so I cut him." Was your question interrogation? Yes. Was the statement made by someone who was in custody? No. So does *Miranda* apply? Certainly not.

Or suppose you are the follow-up officer in the stabbing incident and you're asked to transport the suspect to the station. Enroute, he says to you, "That's not the first asshole

I've used my knife on. You'd think those guys would learn to leave me alone." Was the suspect in custody? Yes. Was his statement a response to interrogation? No. Does *Miranda* apply? It does not.

Where an undercover officer posing as a fellow inmate questions an uncharged prisoner who has not previously invoked his *Miranda* rights, no warning need be given. Since the prisoner would be unaware that he was being questioned by police, he would not experience the coercive effect that *Miranda* warning are designed to neutralize. *Illinois v. Perkins.*

Only when you get affirmative answers to both questions — custody and interrogation — do you need to *Mirandize*. Now, isn't that easier than trying to memorize a bunch of rules?

*Chapter 6*

# GIVING THE WARNING

If you find in applying the Supreme Court's definitions that you do in fact have a custodial interrogation situation, *what* exactly do you have to do to satisfy *Miranda*?

> Prior to any questioning, the person must be warned that he has a right to remain silent, that any statement he does make may be used as evidence against him, and that he has a right to the presence of an attorney, either retained or appointed.
>
> *Miranda*, at 444

There are dozens of variations on the *Miranda* warning, but as long as the wording conveys the information above, it should be sufficient. In *California v. Prysock*, the Supreme Court held that the warning is not required to be a verbatim recitation of the language of *Miranda*:

> This court has never indicated that the
> rigidity of *Miranda* extends to the precise
> formulation of the warnings given a criminal
> defendant....Quite the contrary. *Miranda* it-
> self indicated that no talismanic incantation
> was required to satisfy its strictures.
>
> *California v. Prysock*

*When* do you have to *Mirandize*? Some officers seem to think it's necessary the moment they hook up the crook in the field. Not only is it not legally necessary to do this under the Supreme Court's decisions, it's probably an unwise tactic (see Chapter 13). Under the decisions, it isn't necessary to *Mirandize* until you're ready to begin questioning:

> The principles announced today deal with
> the protection which must be given to the
> privilege against self-incrimination when the
> individual is first subjected to police interro-
> gation while in custody at the station or
> otherwise deprived of his freedom of action
> in any significant way.
>
> *Miranda*, at 477

*Who* has to be *Mirandized*? Anyone, adult or juvenile, who is going to be questioned while in custody. If your suspect is a judge or a lawyer, you still have to *Mirandize*. If the suspect tells you he already knows his rights, you still have to *Mirandize*. If you've arrested and *Mirandized* the same suspect a dozen times before, you still have to *Mirandize*:

> ...we will not pause to inquire in individual
> cases whether the defendant was aware of his
> rights without a warning being given. As-

> sessments of the knowledge the defendant
> possessed, based on information as to his age,
> education, intelligence, or prior contact with
> authorities, can never be more than specula-
> tion; a warning is a clear-cut fact....a warning
> is indispensable....
>
> *Miranda*, at 468

*How often* do you have to give the warning? Some officers seem to think they have to give a new warning every time they take a break and then resume interrogation. No such approach has been required by the Supreme Court, however. Again, why wave the red flag of danger before the suspect's eyes unnecessarily? If you keep reminding the suspect of his rights, he may eventually begin to realize he would be better off shutting his mouth and demanding an attorney.

There aren't any clear-cut guidelines on how often a new *Miranda* warning has to be given, but in the case of *Wyrick v. Fields*, the Supreme Court held that it was unnecessary for a second *Miranda* warning to be given to a suspect before questioning which followed 2 hours of polygraph examination (the suspect had waived his rights at the start of the polygraph). The court said,

> ...the question put to Fields after the ex-
> amination would not have caused him to
> forget the rights of which he had been advised
> and which he understood [when the poly-
> graph exam began].
>
> *Wyrick v. Fields*

*"A heavy burden rests on the government to demonstrate that
the defendant knowingly and intelligently waived his rights. "*
                                                    *Miranda v. Arizona*

The California Supreme Court interprets the need for warnings this way:

> A *Miranda* warning is not required before each custodial interrogation; one warning, if adequately and contemporaneously given, is sufficient.
>
> *People v. Braeseke*

In the California case, the suspect was re-interviewed 1 1/2 hours after the first warning had been given, and this was held sufficient.

In the absence of more definite guidelines from the US Supreme Court, you would probably be well-advised to repeat the warnings before re-interviewing on a subsequent day, but probably need not repeat the warning for successive interviews on the same day.

However, if the suspect refused to waive his rights at the first or any subsequent warning, his rights must be "scrupulously honored," and he cannot be asked at a later time to reconsider and give up his rights with respect to the same period of custody and the same investigation.

In *Michigan v. Mosley*, a suspect who refused to waive his rights as to the case he was arrested on was contacted 2 hours later by an officer from a different agency, concerning a different investigation. This second officer told Mosley he was investigating an unrelated crime, read him his rights, and obtained a waiver and incriminating statements. The Supreme Court held that since the police had scrupulously honored the suspect's initial invocation of his rights, the subsequent waiver was valid, and the statements were admissible.

However, if the suspect requests an *attorney*, no further questioning can occur — as to any crime — until an attorney is provided.

*(Arizona v. Roberson; Edwards v. Arizona)*

To date, the Supreme Court has recognized one exception to the rule that a suspect in custody be *Mirandized* before any questions. This is the "public safety" exception.

In *New York v. Quarles*, an armed rape suspect was chased into a supermarket, where he hid his gun before police captured him. After being handcuffed (and therefore in custody), Quarles was asked, "Where is the gun?" He pointed it out to officers, and then was given a *Miranda* warning. In creating a public safety exception to *Miranda* and holding Quarles' statements admissible against him, the Supreme Court said,

> ...we do not believe that the doctrinal underpinnings of *Miranda* require that it be applied in all its rigor to a situation in which police officers ask questions reasonably prompted by a concern for the public safety.

> We conclude that the need for answers to questions in a situation posing a threat to the public safety outweighs the need for the prophylactic rule protecting the Fifth Amendment's privilege against self-incrimination.

> *New York v. Quarles*

Therefore, anytime you have a public safety threat (such as a loaded gun accessible to others, explosive devices, toxic or hazardous spills, etc.), you should be able to conduct limited questioning of a suspect in custody to neutralize the danger before the need to *Mirandize* attaches. Be sure to document in your report the facts and chronology to support the public safety exception (see further discussion in Chapter 15).

Although there are no US cases defining a "rescue" exception to *Miranda*, there are state court decisions holding that custodial questions may be asked without *Mirandizing* where life is imperiled, as in kidnap cases. For example, where officers in California questioned a kidnapper at the ransom site in order to find out where the victim was being held and how to rescue her from the accomplice, the court of appeal held the answers admissible, without *Miranda* warnings:

> While life hangs in the balance, there is no room to require admonitions concerning the right to counsel and to remain silent.
> *People v. Dean*

Similarly, where officers thought a missing woman left for dead in a remote area might still be alive, the incriminating statements made by the suspect without *Miranda* compliance were allowed:

> ...under circumstances of extreme emergency where the possibility of saving the life of a missing victim exists, noncoercive questions may be asked of a material witness in custody, even though the answers may in-

> criminate the witness. Any other policy would
> reflect indifference to human life.
>
> *People v. Riddle*

Now that we've examined *who* has to be *Mirandized, how* the warnings are to be given, how *often* the same suspect has to have them repeated, and when the warnings can be excused, let's examine *who* has to administer the warnings, and who doesn't.

The Supreme Court has held that the restrictions imposed by the Constitution are restrictions on the powers of government. And in creating the *Miranda* warnings, the court was fashioning a balancing device to combat the inherently compelling influences of official custodial interrogation.

It follows, therefore, that *Miranda* warnings need only be given by governmental officials (such as police and investigators) and their agents, but *not* by private citizens. Thus, a storekeeper who makes a citizen's arrest of a shoplifter has no duty to warn the arrestee of his rights, but may question him fully before the arrival of the police and may obtain admissible incriminating answers.

Likewise, private security guards, employment supervisors and the parents of juvenile offenders all fit into the unofficial category, even though they may occupy positions of authority over some suspect. They need not give a *Miranda* warning before questioning a person they've placed in custody under citizen's arrest. On the other hand, once a police officer arrives on the scene and takes charge, any questioning by the civilian authority figure might be deemed by a court to be the act of a police agent, subject to *Miranda*.

Once a suspect in custody has been given an adequate warning, he may do one of three things: he may waive his rights and agree to discuss the case, he may invoke his rights and refuse to discuss the case, or he may vacillate uncertainly, perhaps asking the officer for clarification of his situation and his options. How do you handle these last two possible responses? We consider these issues next.

*Chapter 7*

# INVOKING

Although the *Miranda* warning was devised to protect the suspect's Fifth Amendment right to silence, it also includes a corresponding right to counsel. Since there are really two rights involved, there are two ways a suspect can prevent interrogation after warning: he can say or do something to invoke his *right to remain silent*, or he can say or do something to invoke his *right to a lawyer* before proceeding:

> Once warnings have been given, the subsequent procedure is clear. If the individual indicates in any manner, at any time prior to or during questioning, that he wishes to remain silent, the interrogation must cease.... If the individual states that he wants an attorney, the interrogation must cease until an attorney is present.
>
> *Miranda*, at 474

The reason it's necessary for you to notice this double-barreled feature of *Miranda* is because a suspect may sometimes say or do something which clearly isn't an invocation of the right to *silence*, but might be an invocation of the right to an *attorney*, or vice versa. If you're only looking at one of these rights you might decide to proceed with an interrogation that the court would later invalidate on the basis of the other right.

For example, suppose you *Mirandize* a juvenile, who happens to be on probation for a prior offense, and after the warning, he tells you he would like to consult with his probation officer. Is he invoking?

The Supreme Court has held that a probation officer is not an attorney and cannot serve the same protective function as an attorney, and therefore a request to consult with a probation officer is *not* an invocation of the right to *counsel*.

On the other hand, the court has pointed out that a juvenile's request for a probation officer (or for his parents) might be the juvenile's way of invoking his right to remain *silent*:

> Where the age and experience of a juvenile indicate that his request for his probation officer or his parents is, in fact, an invocation of his right to remain silent, the totality approach will allow the court the necessary flexibility to take this into account in making a waiver determination.
>
> *Fare v. Michael C.*

So the first thing to notice about the issue of whether or not you have a suspect who's invoking his rights is that you have to consider his response first from the standpoint of the right to remain silent, and then with respect to his right to a lawyer.

The next thing to remember is that not only are there two *rights* involved in *Miranda*, there are also two separate *issues* to be resolved before interrogation proceeds:

(1) has there been an *invocation*, and

(2) has there been a *waiver*?

> Invocation and waiver are entirely distinct inquiries, and the two must not be blurred by merging them together.
>
> *Smith v. Illinois*

So before you start testing the suspect's responses to your warning against the requirements for a valid *waiver*, you should first check to see if his responses amount to an *invocation*.

Some cases, of course, are easy. You ask the suspect if he understands his rights, and he gives you an unequivocal "Yes." You ask if he wants to give up his rights and discuss the case, and you get another "Yes." Answers like these dispose of the invocation and waiver issues both at the same time.

The difficulty comes with ambiguous responses, like these:

*"I don't know what I should do."*

*"What would you do if you were me?"*

*"I know I'm going to need a lawyer before this thing's over."*

*"I guess it would be better if I didn't say anything right now."*

Remember that in *Rhode Island v. Innis*, the Supreme Court defined interrogation and its functional equivalent as conduct by the police which they should reasonably know is likely to evoke an *incriminating* response. Therefore, this is the *only* kind of conduct or questioning that is prohibited in the absence of a waiver. You may still ask other questions, incident to the suspect's custody, which are not likely to elicit self-incrimination.

One such category of questions is that intended to *clarify* the suspect's position. If his response to the warning is ambiguous, rather than assume that he is not invoking his rights, it's better to ask clarifying questions to establish as clearly as possible whether he really is invoking his rights.

For example, in *Smith v. Illinois*, the officer began to advise the suspect of his rights, and when he asked Smith if he understood the right to remain silent, Smith replied, "Uh. She told me to get my lawyer. She said you guys would railroad me."

Instead of stopping at this point to clarify whether Smith understood his right to remain silent and was invoking his right to an attorney, the officer continued with the *Miranda* warning. Smith eventually agreed to talk and made incriminating statements.

In ruling Smith's statements inadmissible, the Supreme Court found that Smith had attempted to invoke his right to an attorney, after having been advised by the officer that he could have one, by saying, "Uh, yeah. I'd like to do that." Since the officer failed to cease questioning at that point, the statements he obtained were in violation of *Miranda* and couldn't be used.

Instead of ignoring a suspect's ambiguous responses and plowing ahead with the standard *Miranda* warning, as the officer in *Smith* improperly did, it's better to stop and explain the rights further, if the suspect indicates he doesn't understand them. It's also better to stop and give the suspect clear-cut choices to try to get an unequivocal response. (For instance, the officer in *Smith* might have followed up the suspect's comment by saying, "Mr. Smith, I need to be sure I understand what you want. Are you asking for an attorney right now, before we go any further, or are you just saying that you're going to want an attorney later? It's your choice and right either way.")

Contrast the situation in *Davis v. US.* In that case, the suspect initially gave an unambiguous waiver and began to answer questions. Later, he said, "Maybe I should talk to a lawyer." The Supreme Court ruled that this statement was not a clear-cut, unambiguous invocation of Davis's rights, and since he had already waived, the burden shifted to him to clearly assert his rights if he chose to do so. The interrogating officers were under no duty to cease questioning or to clarify Davis's wishes, once he had waived his rights.

Another recurring issue with invocations is whether or not a suspect can abandon his initial invocation by reinitiating discussions with police. Suppose after you give a suspect a complete *Miranda* warning he clearly tells you he wants to remain silent. Then, as you're taking him back to his cell, he tells you he has changed his mind about talking and wants to tell you his side of the story. What should you do?

The Supreme Court also considered this possibility in the *Smith* case:

> ...if the accused invoked his right to counsel, courts may admit his responses to further questioning only on finding that he (a) initiated further discussions with police and (b) knowingly and intelligently waived the right he had invoked.
>
> *Smith v. Illinois*

What you should do in such a situation, therefore, is to remind the suspect of the right he had invoked (silence or attorney), and ask him if he has changed his mind and now wants to give up that right and to discuss the case. Be sure your report clearly shows that it was the *suspect* who reinitiated conversation, and that he knowingly and intelligently waived his rights (see discussion of waiver in the next chapter, and report-writing pointers in Chapter 14).

A good example of reinitiation occurred where a manslaughter suspect, when advised of his rights, said "I do want an attorney before it goes very much further." The officer treated this statement as an invocation of the right to counsel and ceased discussions. Sometime later, while the suspect was being taken to county jail, he asked the officer, "Well, what is going to happen to me now?"

The officer reminded the suspect that he had requested an attorney and told him there was no need to talk "unless you so desire." The suspect said he understood, and the officer told him what the charges were and where he was being taken, and suggested that a polygraph exam might be useful. The suspect agreed, and eventually signed a written waiver, took the polygraph, and made admissions.

The Supreme Court approved the officer's handling of this case, based on the test set out in *Smith*. Said the court:

> Although ambiguous, the respondent's question in this case as to what was going to happen to him evinced a willingness and a desire for a generalized discussion about the investigation.
> *Oregon v. Bradshaw*

The court also pointed out that once an accused has invoked his rights, there may still be exchanges between him and police which are "routine incidents of custody," such as jail processing, use of the telephone, etc. Comments from the suspect along these lines would not generally amount to a reinitiation of discussions about the investigation, but you should be alert to the possibility that the suspect may ask a question like the one in *Oregon v. Bradshaw* which "evinces a willingness" to talk about the case.

In *McNeil v. Wisconsin*, the Supreme Court said, in a footnote, that because Miranda rights do not arise until the onset of custodial interrogation, they may not be invoked "anticipatorily," in advance. This means that a suspect who is not in custody, or not facing police interrogation, does not necessarily invoke Miranda by asking for an attorney or declaring a refusal to speak.

There's one final point on invocation, and although it's a fine point which might never arise in everyday police work, you might want to be aware of it. The Supreme Court has left open the possibility that even after a suspect invokes his right to remain silent, permissible questioning might still take place, provided the suspect's attorney is present:

> If an individual indicates his desire to remain silent, but has an attorney present, there may be some circumstances in which further questioning would be permissible. In the absence

*"In this case, no evidence at all was introduced to prove that petitioner knowingly and intelligently waived his rights. The statement was, therefore, inadmissible"*

*Tague v. Louisiana*

> of evidence of overbearing, statements then
> made in the presence of counsel might be free
> of the compelling influence of the interrogation
> process and might fairly be construed as a
> waiver of the privilege for purposes of these
> statements.
>
> *Miranda*, Fn.44

Unfortunately, the court did not specify what kinds of circumstances would permit continued questioning following an invocation of the right to remain silent. The most likely things are the kinds of circumstances which excuse *Miranda* —public safety and rescue situations. If you ever have those situations and your suspect has invoked, it might be a good idea to get him a lawyer and continue to question him (no overbearing or badgering) with the lawyer present, and rely on footnote 44 in court.

If your suspect in any given case does *not* invoke either his right to remain silent or his right to an attorney, the next step is to see whether he is effectively *waiving* these rights, so that interrogation can begin.

*Chapter 8*

# WAIVER

In order to get a crook's statement into evidence, it isn't enough just to show that he was adequately warned of his rights and that he did nothing to invoke them — it's also necessary to show that you obtained a valid *waiver* of the rights to silence and counsel:

> ...the individual may knowingly and intelligently waive these rights and agree to answer questions or make a statement. But unless and until such warnings and waiver are demonstrated by the prosecution at trial, no evidence obtained as a result of interrogation can be used against him.
>
> *Miranda*, at 479

This brief passage from *Miranda* has three significant provisions:

(1)   the burden of proving a waiver is on the prosecution;

(2) that a suspect waived his rights has to be "demon strated" somehow to the court; and

(3) any waiver has to be "knowing and intelligent" (an additional requirement that the waiver be "voluntary" was imposed earlier in the *Miranda* deci sion at page 444.)

That the prosecution has to bear the burden of proving a waiver occurred isn't surprising:

> Since the State is responsible for establishing the isolated circumstances under which the interrogation takes place and has the only means of making available corroborated evidence of warnings given during incommunicado interrogation, the burden is rightly on its shoulders.
>
> *Miranda*, at 475

As to the second point — that the existence of a waiver has to be "demonstrated" in court — the Supreme Court meant that a waiver would not be presumed to have occurred simply because the suspect gave no indication he wanted to invoke his rights, or because he ultimately answered questions or made a statement. Something more is required to "demonstrate" a waiver:

> ...a valid waiver will not be presumed simply from the silence of the accused after warnings are given or simply from the fact that a confession was in fact eventually obtained.
>
> *Miranda*, at 475

> With respect to the waiver inquiry, we
> have emphasized that a valid waiver cannot
> be established by showing only that the ac-
> cused responded to further police-initiated
> custodial interrogation.
>
> *Smith v. Illinois*

What would be sufficient to demonstrate a waiver?

> An express statement that the individual is
> willing to make a statement and does not want
> an attorney followed closely by a statement
> could constitute a waiver.
>
> *Miranda,* at 475

So if you have proof that the suspect told you he didn't
want a lawyer and that he was willing to talk, the prosecutor
can "demonstrate" that the suspect waived his rights.

But though an express statement might be the most
logical means of demonstrating a waiver, the Supreme Court
has not ruled out other forms of proof, including an *implied*
waiver, based on the suspect's conduct:

> An express written or oral statement of the
> right to remain silent or of the right to counsel
> is usually strong proof of the validity of that
> waiver, but is not inevitably either necessary
> or sufficient to establish waiver. In at least
> some cases, waiver can be clearly inferred
> from the actions and words of the person
> interrogated.
>
> *North Carolina v. Butler*

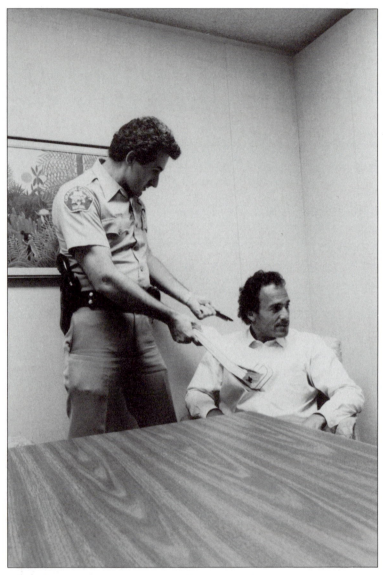

*"Use by a state of an improperly obtained confession may constitute a denial of due process of law as guaranteed by the Fourteenth Amendment."*

*Chambers v. Florida*

For example, suppose you advise a suspect of his rights and ask him whether he's willing to give up his rights and talk to you about the case. Instead of answering "yes" and thereby giving you an express waiver, he says, "I'm gonna tell you what happened, in my own way, before I start answering your questions," and then he proceeds to do so. A court would most likely find an implied waiver in a case like this, following *North Carolina v. Butler*.

The third point from the *Miranda* discussion of waivers is that demonstrable proof of a waiver has to be such as to show that the accused gave the waiver "voluntarily, knowingly and intelligently." How do you satisfy this requirement?

A waiver is voluntary, in the legal sense, when it results from the suspect's exercise of his own free will; it is not voluntary if it was brought about by any inducement or improper influence:

> ...any evidence that the accused was threatened, tricked, or cajoled into a waiver will, of course, show that the defendant did not voluntarily waive his privilege.
>
> *Miranda*, at 476

What did this passage say? You cannot *threaten* the suspect to get him to waive his rights. His waiver will not be voluntary if you first told him that things would go hard on him if he refused to talk, or that his wife would have to be arrested, or that he would look guilty if he remained silent, or that you would treat him as an uncooperative prisoner, etc. Any express or implied threats about the consequences of his not waiving his rights will make any waiver you obtain

involuntary — and any resulting statements inadmissible —
as a matter of law.

You cannot *trick* the suspect into waiving his rights.
Although it's usually permissible to trick him into confessing *after* you get a valid waiver (see tactics in Chapter 13),
you cannot use any deception or tricks *before* obtaining the
waiver.

You cannot *cajole* the suspect into a waiver. This means
you cannot use any express or implied promises of reward or
leniency to prompt a waiver; do not promise better jailhouse
conditions, a more favorable report, more favorable testimony, a lighter sentence, lower bail, or any other such
incentive to make the suspect waive his rights. Also, you
cannot "soften up" the suspect before advisement and waiver
by telling him how much you sympathize with him, or how
awful his victim was, or how justifiable his crime was in
comparison with others you've seen, etc. Any such "cajol-
ing" *prior* to waiver will invalidate the waiver.

(All of this does *not* necessarily mean, however, that
you can't make a legitimate difference in whether or not your
suspect decides, of his own free will, to give up his rights and
talk to you. Your timing and technique can considerably
improve your chances of getting a waiver, within lawful
bounds, in many cases, as discussed in Chapter 13.)

In addition to being "voluntary," a suspect's waiver also
has to be "knowing and intelligent." This basically means
that he has to be aware of the consequences of a waiver (that
his statements will be used against him in court, as stated in
the warning), and that he appears to have been sufficiently
intelligent and alert to comprehend the meaning of his rights
and the consequences of his decision to waive them. While
this doesn't mean you have to give every suspect an IQ test
before taking a waiver, it does mean that if the circumstances

of the crime or the interrogation suggest any kind of possible impairment (intoxication, drugs, youthful age, injury, lack of sleep, subnormal intelligence, language problem, etc.), you should take steps to seal off an unwarranted defense effort to invalidate the waiver.

For example, you might consider having the suspect tell you what the rights mean, in his own words, and record his comments. Or, have him write his understanding of his rights on a piece of paper, and then ask him to write out his decision about whether or not he chooses to talk to you. These safeguards are not necessary, of course, where there are no indications of comprehension difficulty and an intelligent waiver appears from the context of the interrogation — but keep in mind that the prosecution has the burden of proving a valid waiver, somehow.

The issue of whether or not a valid waiver has been obtained was analyzed by the Supreme Court in a case where the suspect was in custody and, unknown to him, an attorney had called police and instructed them not to question the suspect. Could police, without telling the suspect about the attorney's call, still obtain a valid waiver and an admissible statement?

> The inquiry has two distinct dimensions. First, the relinquishment of the right must have been voluntary in the sense that it was the product of a free and deliberate choice rather than intimidation, coercion or deception. Second, the waiver must have been made with a full awareness both of the nature of the right being abandoned and the consequences of the decision to abandon it. Only if the totality of the circumstances surrounding

the interrogation reveal both an uncoerced choice and the requisite level of comprehension may a court properly conclude that the *Miranda* rights have been waived.

*Moran v. Burbine*

Reasoning that Burbine's lack of knowledge that a lawyer had called and told police not to interrogate him could not have affected his ability to comprehend his rights or to freely choose to waive them, the Supreme Court ruled that the waiver was valid. In a footnote, the Court also noted that the right to remain silent could not be invoked by an attorney on his client's behalf, but only by the client himself:

...the privilege against compulsory self-incrimination is, by hypothesis, a personal one that can only be invoked by the individual whose testimony is being compelled.

*Moran v. Burbine*, Fn.4

The Supreme Court has also held that a valid waiver can be obtained from a suspect, even though he was mistakenly questioned briefly without warnings when warnings should have been given — provided such questioning was not coercive in nature. A policeman serving an arrest warrant at the suspect's home asked him two or three questions about his knowledge of the crime; the suspect answered, implicating himself. Later, the suspect was *Mirandized* and waived his rights. Although the initial answers violated *Miranda* and had to be suppressed, they did not prevent a valid waiver following proper warnings:

We hold today that a suspect who has once responded to unwarned yet uncoercive questioning is not thereby disabled from waiving his rights and confessing after he has been given the requisite *Miranda* warnings.

*Oregon v. Elstad*

Since the prosecution has the burden of proving that adequate warnings were given and a valid waiver was obtained, methods of insuring that the prosecutor will be able to meet this burden are covered in Chapter 14. Remember that a waiver will not be presumed by the court, and therefore cannot be presumed by the interrogator. Before you begin to ask questions of your suspect, be sure to ask *yourself* what the suspect has said and done to effect a waiver, and how you'll be able to prove the waiver in court, if necessary.

# Chapter 9

# INTERROGATION AND THE 6TH AMENDMENT

## The Right to Counsel

The third test of the Constitutional admissibility of a suspect's statement is whether or not it was obtained in violation of the Sixth Amendment:

> In all criminal prosecutions, the accused
> shall enjoy the right...to have the Assistance
> of Counsel for his defense.

Two years before issuing the *Miranda* decision interpreting *Fifth* Amendment rights, the Supreme Court had already twice applied an exclusionary rule to suppress statements obtained through police practices the Court found to violate the *Sixth* Amendment.

The first of these involved a narcotics investigation that was still under way, even after the suspect had been arrested and arraigned, had hired a lawyer, and had been released on bail, awaiting trial. Investigators wired the suspect's codefendant and listened in on street conversations between the two, and later testified at trial to statements they had overheard. The Supreme Court ruled these statements inadmissible.

Even though the language of the Sixth Amendment quoted above talks about the assistance of counsel in criminal "prosecutions," and though this had usually been understood to mean during *courtroom proceedings*, the Court concluded that the right to counsel should attach as soon as an individual became "the accused." Obviously, once the suspect had been charged and arraigned, he was "the accused," and the efforts of investigators to obtain statements from him after that point were impermissible, unless his attorney were present:

> We hold that the petitioner was denied the basic protections of the Sixth Amendment guarantee when there was used against him at his trial evidence of his own incriminating words, which federal agents had deliberately elicited from him after he had been indicted and in the absence of his counsel.
>
> *Massiah v. United States*

The next case to which the Supreme Court applied a Sixth Amendment exclusionary theory was *Escobedo v. Illinois*. Danny Escobedo was subjected to custodial interrogation about a murder, in spite of his repeated requests for his attorney (who was present in the station house, demanding to see his client). Since the interrogation took place two years before the *Miranda* decision, officers had not advised Escobedo of his rights nor obtained any waivers. Escobedo confessed.

The Supreme Court held that under all of these circumstances, Escobedo had been denied the assistance of counsel, "and that no statement elicited by the police during the interrogation may be used against him at a criminal trial."

The kindest thing that can be said about the *Escobedo* opinion, written by Justice Goldber, is that it was unfortunate. The opinion was not well-reasoned: it overlooked the fact that Danny Escobedo had not been charged, nor booked, nor indicted, nor arraigned; in other words, by the Supreme Court's own test, he had not become "the accused," and so his Sixth Amendment right had not attached. If it had not attached, how could it have been violated?

What the Court had apparently wanted to do in *Escobedo* it eventually did two years later in *Miranda*, when it reached the same result by holding that such custodial interrogations violated the *Fifth* Amendment privilege against compulsory self-incrimination. The Supreme Court itself subsequently acknowledge the flaw in *Escobedo*:

> Although Escobedo was originally decided as a Sixth Amendment case, the Court in retrospect perceived that the prime purpose of Escobedo was not vindicate the constitutional right to counsel as such, but, like *Miranda*, to guarantee full effectuation of the privilege against self-incrimination.

* * *

> ...the Sixth Amendment right to counsel does not attach until after the initiation of formal charges.
> 
> *Moran v. Burbine*

Although this discussion of the rationale of *Escobedo* may seem a little academic to you, it's necessary for law enforcement personnel concerned with the admissibility of confessions to be aware that (1) *Escobedo* is the only Supreme Court decision applying a Sixth Amendment restriction to the interrogation of an *uncharged* suspect, and (2) this holding has *not* been followed in later Sixth Amendment decisions and has, in fact, been expressly disavowed.

The rule, instead, is that for interrogation purposes,

> ...a person's Sixth Amendment right to counsel attaches only at or after the time that adversary judicial proceedings have been initiated against him...whether by way of formal charge, preliminary hearing, indictment, information or arraignment.
>
> *US v. Gouveia*

In the years since *Massiah* and *Escobedo*, the Supreme Court has generally reviewed post-indictment interrogations from a Sixth Amendment viewpoint, and has considered issues relating to counsel in pre-indictment interrogations from a Fifth Amendment/*Miranda* point of view.

For example, Robert Edwards had not yet been indicted or arraigned when he was questioned, in custody, about a robbery-homicide he was suspected of committing. He first waived *Miranda*, and later said he wanted an attorney before talking further. Officers returned Edwards to his cell, but returned the nest day for more questioning. The re-advised Edwards and took a new "waiver," eventually getting some incriminating admissions.

On the basis of *Miranda* and the Fifth Amendment, the Supreme Court invalidated the second waiver:

...when an accused has invoked his right to have counsel present during custodial interrogation, a valid waiver of that right cannot be established by showing only that he responded to further police-initiated custodial interrogation even if he has been advised of his rights. We further hold that an accused, such as Edwards, having expressed his desire to deal with the police only through counsel, is not subject to further interrogation by the authorities until counsel has been made available to him, unless the accused himself initiates further communication, exchanges, or conversations with the police.

*Edwards v. Arizona*

In other words, once a suspect in custody says he wants a lawyer, you cannot obtain a legally valid waiver for further interrogation without a lawyer, unless the suspect himself re-opens discussions with you. But this is not a result of the Sixth Amendment clause on "assistance of counsel"; it is because of *Miranda's* recognition of the role an attorney can play in safeguarding a suspect's right against compelled self-incrimination:

The Fifth Amendment right identified in *Miranda* is the right to have counsel present at any custodial interrogation.

*Edwards v. Arizona*

Contrast the case of Robert Williams, a murder suspect who had been arrested, arraigned, and released to the custody of officers for transportation to the jurisdiction of the crime.

Williams was represented by an attorney, and he told the transporting officer she would not discuss the case with them until he had seen his attorney. The officers nevertheless obtained incriminating statements from Williams as thy drive him back to their jurisdiction. The Court applied the post-indictment Six the Amendment test;

> ...the right to counsel granted by the Sixth Amendment means at least that a person is entitled to the help of a lawyer at or after the time that judicial proceeding have been initiated against him — whether by way of formal charge, preliminary hearing, indictment, information or arraignment.
>
> *Brewer v. Williams*

Calling the police conduct a "clear violation" of Williams's Sixth Amendment rights, the Supreme Court suppressed his statements and granted his writ of habeas corpus on charges of murdering a young girl. (Imagine being the police officer who had to explain this turn of events to the girl's parents, and you should have no difficulty appreciating the necessity of understanding all of the case law in interrogation — not just *Miranda*.)

And just as the Court had done in *Edwards v. Arizona* as the waivers of counsel in *Fifth* Amendment contexts by uncharged suspects, it held in a later case that the *Sixth* Amendment right to counsel for accused persons could no longer be waived, once invoked, merely by police officers giving a new *Miranda* warning and soliciting a new "waiver:"

> Just as written waivers are insufficient to justify police-initiated interrogations after the

request for counsel in a Fifth Amendment analysis, so too they are insufficient to justify police-initiated interrogations after the request for counsel in a Sixth Amendment analysis.

\* \* \*

We hold that, if police initiate interrogation after a defendant's assertion, at an arraignment or other proceeding, of his right to counsel, any waiver of the defendant's right to counsel for that police-initiated interrogation is invalid.

*Michigan v. Jackson*

Again, the Supreme Court left open the possibility that the accused could change his mind and waive the presence of counsel, but only if he himself independently decided to initiate renewed discussions with police.

Taken together, then, *Edwards* and *Jackson* yield the following general rule: *once a suspect is in custody or has been formally charged, if he requests an attorney, he can be questioned further only if the prosecution can prove that the suspect volunteered to talk, and can prove that the suspect knowingly relinquished his right to counsel.*

(Note that asserting the right to counsel is not the same thing as invoking the right to remain silent. The case of *Michigan v. Mosley*, previously discussed in Chapter 6, held that officers from a different agency, investigating a different crime, could obtain a valid waiver from a suspect who had refused to waive his right to silence in an earlier, unrelated investigation.)

Two additional features of Sixth Amendment case law require attention. One is that an accused's right to the assistance of counsel can be violated not only by open and obvious interrogation, but also by bugging, eavesdropping, or contact by an informant.

For example, where a defendant had been indicted and was being held in jail awaiting trial, the use of a "jailhouse snitch" to overhear and report on the defendant's remarks about his participation in a robbery was ruled impermissible, even though the snitch had been told not to engage in any direct questioning of the defendant:

> By intentionally creating a situation likely to induce Henry to make incriminating statements without the assistance of counsel, the Government violated Henry's Sixth Amendment right to counsel.
>
> *US v. Henry*

Similarly, in a case where a defendant had been arraigned and released pending trial, with an attorney retained, the decision by police to wire the codefendant and record conversations was held to result in a Sixth Amendment violation:

> ...The prosecutor and police have an affirmative obligation not to act in a manner that circumvents and thereby dilutes the protection afforded by the right to counsel.

* * *

> ...knowing exploitation by the State of an opportunity to confront the accused without

> counsel being present is as much a breach of
> the State's obligation not to circumvent the
> right to the assistance of counsel as is the
> intentional creation of such an opportunity.
>
> *Maine v. Moulton*

These rulings essentially mean that once the right to counsel has attached and been asserted, police cannot initiate any interrogation — whether custodial or noncustodial — and cannot use undercover officers, informants, or other agents or devices to obtain statements from the accused. Of course the accused himself can still waive the presence of counsel and volunteer statements, and police can use any statements come by without any "knowing exploitation" of an interrogation opportunity:

> Thus, the Sixth Amendment is not violated
> whenever — by luck or happenstance — the
> State obtains incriminating statements from
> the accused after the right to counsel has
> attached.
>
> *Maine v. Moulton*

The remaining feature of the decisional law on Sixth Amendment restrictions on interrogations is that it's possible for an officer to violate the right to counsel, even without realizing that the suspect he's talking to has been formally charged, or without knowing the suspect has asserted his right to counsel at an arraignment or other proceeding. The Supreme Court has taken the position that all law enforcement officers and all prosecutors, representing the State, are chargeable with knowing what any one of them *or the court* knows about the accused's status, and with acting accordingly:

*Robber's sixty-five year sentence reversed due to police error.*

> Sixth Amendment principles require that we impute the State's knowledge from one state actor to another. For the Sixth Amendment concerns the confrontation between the State and the individual. One set of state actors (the police) may not claim ignorance of defendants' unequivocal request for counsel to another state actor (the court)
>
> *Michigan v. Jackson*

If you're about ready at this point for a short summary of the distinction between Fifth and Sixth Amendment rights to counsel, this final quotation from the *Jackson* decision may help:

> The existence of that right is clear. It has two sources. The Fifth Amendment protection against compelled self-incrimination provides the right to counsel at custodial interrogations. The Sixth Amendment guarantee of the assistance of counsel also provides the right to counsel at postarraignment interrogations. The arraignment signals the initiation of adversary judicial proceedings and thus the attachment of the Sixth Amendment; thereafter, government efforts to elicit information from the accused, including *interrogation, represent "critical stages" at which the Sixth Amendment applies.*
>
> *Michigan v. Jackson*

Now that you've taken the time to work you way through this discussion of interrogation and the Sixth Amendment, several points should probably occur to you:

- It's possible for a police officer to violate the Sixth Amendment right to counsel and render a confession inadmissible in evidence, even though he has a signed *Miranda* waiver, or even though *Miranda* doesn't apply. For example, interrogation of an accused who is out on bail (or OR) isn't subject to *Miranda*, since the accused is not "in custody" during the interrogation; however, this interrogation is subject to *Massiah*, and so it's allowable only if the accused initiates it and relinquishes his right to the presence of counsel.

- After the right to counsel has attached, but *before* the accused asserts it, a *Miranda* waiver would be adequate to waive the presence of counsel for any discussions the accused chooses to engage in. This was essentially the situation — and the holding — in *Patterson v. Illinois*, in which the Supreme Court ruled an indicted murder suspect's statement admissible because he waived and *had not asserted* his right to an attorney.

- Since you are chargeable under the "state agent" theory with knowing whether or not your interrogation subject has previously asserted his right to counsel, it might be advisable to ask every suspect, during the course of taking standard "*Miranda* waivers," whether he's currently under any indictments or charges anywhere, and whether he is represented by an attorney or has made a request for one.

- Whenever possible, you'll want to complete your interrogation of a suspect *before* he has been formally charged, indicted or arraigned.

- However, the issuance of a criminal complaint and arrest warrant will not necessarily trigger the Sixth Amendment, before the accused is indicted or arraigned. Therefore, if you arrest a suspect on complaint/warrant, only *Miranda* (not *Massiah*) will apply before arraignment. You may seek a *Miranda* waiver and interrogate, without violating the *Jackson* rule. (See *Pace v. US.*)

- In any instance in which a suspect or an accused does initiate renewed interrogation, *Edwards* and *Jackson* make it imperative that you preserve the best possible proof (tape recording or writing — not just verbal assurances) that the suspect voluntarily reinitiated and executed whatever form of waiver of counsel your jurisdiction requires.

- As a rule of thumb on jailhouse informants, if a fellow prisoner comes to you on his own and tells you something he happened to overhear, it's probably admissible; if you send him back in to keep his ears open and he reports back with something more, that new statement is probably inadmissible (provided the confessor's Fifth or Sixth Amendment right to counsel has attached), unless the statement relates to a *planned* crime or an *uncharged* crime.

**Recap:** Whereas *Miranda* advisements and waivers relate only to "custodial interrogation" of any suspect — charged or uncharged — the Sixth Amendment right to counsel is not limited to "custodial" interrogation and includes undercover questioning and surreptitious recording of suspects in or out of custody — but only if they've been formally charged somehow. Once a suspect has invoked either his Fifth or Sixth Amendment right to counsel, only the suspect himself — and not the police — may initiate new waiver discussions and interrogation. Emphasizing that *Miranda*'s right to counsel applies to any interrogation on any case as long as the suspect is in *custody*, and that the Sixth Amendment right to counsel apples only to cases that have been formally charged in court, the Supreme Court has refused to consider an invocation of either right as an automatic invocation of the other. *McNeil v. Wisconsin.* Instead, the two rights must be analyzed separately, each according to its own unique rules.

*Chapter 10*

# INTERROGATION AND THE 14TH AMENDMENT

## Voluntariness

Most of the case law on suppression of incriminating statements on the basis of *Fourth Amendment* violations dates back to the early 1960s (*Mapp v. Ohio, Wong Sun v. US*). The *Fifth Amendment* cases began with *Miranda* in 1966; and the *Sixth Amendment* exclusionary rule basically began with *Massiah* in 1964.

Because the development of these three sets of exclusionary rules began in relatively recent criminal justice history, most of what you may have heard and read in your law enforcement career about the admissibility of confessions probably was largely concerned with Fourth, Fifth or Sixth Amendment law — principally *Miranda* refinements. Long before the Supreme Court and law enforcement educators became preoccupied with these developing theories, however, there existed a large body of law defining circumstances under which a suspect's statements were inadmissible in evidence as violating the "due process" clause of the *Fourteenth Amendment*.

Many criminal lawyers and judges agree that *today*, a major problem with the admissibility of suspects' statements continues to be the inadvertent violation of the Fourteenth Amendment by officers while obtaining statements. But considering that the Fourteenth Amendment test of admissibility of statements, dating back at least as far as the 1936 decision in *Brown v. Mississippi*, is the oldest of the four constitutional tests and should logically be the best-defined for police officers, why should it continue to cause problems?

The answer may simply be that in their hurry to keep up with the flood of new decisions coming down from the courts applying Fourth, Fifth and Sixth Amendment rules since the 1960s, law enforcement academies and educators may have been forced to neglect the more traditional Fourteenth Amendment area. Or it may be that with the declining use of interrogation as an investigative tool in the wake of *Miranda's* initial confusion, issues of due process were not expected to arise. At least some law enforcement personnel may have mistakenly felt that *Miranda* had "absorbed" all other constitutional issues on admissibility of statements, and that a warning and waiver per *Miranda* could guarantee that a statement would be admissible.

Whatever the reason, it appears from recent case decisions that significant numbers of law enforcement officers either are only vaguely aware, or even are entirely unaware, that no statement they obtain from a criminal suspect is admissible in court unless and until the prosecution proves that it meets due process requirements under the Fourteenth Amendment. Thus, it often comes as a frustrating surprise to officers who were careful in their interrogation to comply with applicable Fourth, Fifth and Sixth Amendment rules, that the confession they obtained is nevertheless inadmissible — and therefore useless — due to their unknowing transgression of Fourteenth Amendment restrictions.

In case *you* may have been among that number of officers not fully informed about the implications of the due process clause, this is a good time to become acquainted with the following facts: a suspect's statement can be found admissible under *Mapp, Wong Sun, Dunaway,* and other Fourth Amendment decisions, and still be inadmissible under the Fourteenth; it can be admissible under *Massiah* and the Sixth Amendment rules, but inadmissible under the Fourteenth; you can have a perfect *Miranda* advisement and waiver to satisfy Fifth Amendment concerns, and still lose your cop-out under the Fourteenth Amendment. Do you know how? Why? When?

As with *Miranda* concepts, understanding the "what, when and why" of due process issues in interrogation will allow you to know how to avoid the standard problems. The Fourteenth Amendment provides, in part,

> No State shall make or enforce any law which shall abridge the privileges or immunities of citizens of the United States; nor shall any State deprive any person of life, liberty, or property, without due process of law.

When a criminal-accused is put on trial, his conviction normally results in a sentence of punishment which may include depriving him of his life (in death-penalty cases), his liberty (if he's committed to jail or to prison), or his property (to the extent of any fines imposed). Therefore, obviously, the due process clause governs every state and federal criminal prosecution (*Malloy v. Hogan*).

But what does due process in a trial have to do with police interrogations? The Supreme Court's analysis goes like this: due process requires that courts admit and rely on only "worthy" evidence — that is, evidence which was collected in such a way that it appears to be *trustworthy*, and that resulted from investigative practices which are *worthy* of our accusatorial, rather than inquisitorial, system of justice. Interrogation practices which are likely to produce unreliable confessions, and those confessions obtained by offensive or oppressive tactics, do not satisfy the worthiness doctrine, or the due process clause.

It's obvious, for example, that if an officer were to physically abuse a suspect in order to get a confession, the confession wouldn't be very reliable evidence: many people would falsely confess to crimes they didn't commit if doing so would bring relief from physical abuse. A conviction based on such a confession would amount to the state depriving the accused of life, liberty or property without due process of law. This is precisely why the Supreme Court reversed a conviction where the confession was obtained by beatings, in *Brown v. Mississippi* (1936).

But physical abuse isn't the only kind of police "pressure" which might produce an unreliable confession. *Threats* of abuse could have the same effect on some persons, as could threats to arrest spouses or children unless the suspect confessed, or threats to increase the degree of the charges or the severity of the punishment for a non-confessing suspect.

Likewise, offers to provide some special *benefit* in exchange for a confession — such as reducing the charges, lowering bail, putting in a good word with the DA or the judge — might prompt an innocent person to confess to a crime he didn't commit.

In these situations and similar others, the suspect's confession would be unreliable, and therefore inadmissible, because it was forcibly obtained or induced by some sort of bargain, rather than coming from the suspect voluntarily due to his consciousness of guilt. Recognizing this basis for refusing to use involuntary confessions as evidence of guilt, the Supreme Court has consistently imposed, since 1897, a *voluntariness* test which statements have to pass before being admitted into evidence:

> It is now inescapably clear that the Fourteenth Amendment forbids the use of involuntary confessions not only because of the probable unreliability of confessions that are obtained in a manner deemed coercive, but also because of the strongly felt attitude of our society that important human values are sacrificed where an agency of the government, in the course of securing a conviction, wrings a confession out of an accused against his will, and because of the deep- rooted feeling that the police must obey the law while enforcing the law.
>
> *Jackson v. Denno*

> This means that a vital confession may go to the jury only if it is subjected to screening in accordance with correct constitutional standards.
>
> *Rogers v. Richmond*

Jackson v. Denno requires judicial rulings on voluntariness prior to admitting confessions.

*　*　*

Thus, the prosecution must prove at least by a preponderance of the evidence that the confession was voluntary.

*Lego v. Twomey*

Determination of whether a statement is involuntary requires careful evaluation of all the circumstances of the interrogation.

*Mincey v. Arizona*

And what is the voluntariness standard to be applied in evaluating the interrogation circumstances?

Is the confession the product of an essentially free and unconstrained choice by its maker? If it is, if he has willed to confess, it may be used against him. If it is not, if his will has been overborne and his capacity for self-determination critically impaired, the use of his confession offends due process.

*Culombe v. Connecticut*

A statement to be voluntary of course need not be volunteered. But if it is the product of sustained pressure by the police it does not issue from a free choice.

*Watts v. Indiana*

A confession may have been given voluntarily, although it was made to police officers, while in custody, and in answer to an examination conducted by them.

*Wan v. US*

These passages from Supreme Court decisions define *three features* of the voluntariness test under the Fourteenth Amendment:

1) a confession can be voluntary even though it was obtained by interrogation — that is, due process does not require that a suspect walk into the station and blurt out his confession before it can be considered voluntary;

2) a suspect's confession is involuntary if police pressures are brought to bear to overcome his will to resist; and

3) a voluntary statement cannot be obtained from a suspect whose capacity to think for himself is critically impaired.

So, skillfully interrogating an evasive, untruthful and defensive suspect is permissible as long as no impermissible tactics are used. Impermissible tactics, as suggested above, could include not only actual or threatened violence, but psychological pressure or offers to bargain for a statement in exchange for some promised benefit:

...the constitutional inquiry is not whether the conduct of state officers in obtaining the confession was shocking, but whether the confession was free and voluntary: that is, it must not be extracted by any sort of threats or violence, nor obtained by any direct or implied promises, however slight, nor by the exertion of any improper influence.

*Bram v. US*

As reflected in the cases in this Court, police conduct requiring exclusion of a confession has evolved from acts of clear physical brutality to more refined and subtle methods of overcoming a defendant's will.

\* \* \*

This Court has recognized that coercion can be mental as well as physical....

*Jackson v. Denno*

Our decisions under the Fourteenth Amendment have made clear that convictions following the admission into evidence of confessions which are involuntary, i.e., the product of coercion, either physical or psychological, cannot stand.

*Rogers v. Richmond*

...any criminal trial use against a defendant of his involuntary statement is a denial of due process of law, even if there is ample evi-

dence aside from the confession to support
the conviction.

*Mincey v. Arizona*

What are some specific examples of police interrogation practices considered by the Court to be overbearing?

● Suspect was physically beaten until he confessed.
*Brown v. Mississippi.*

● Interrogator told a woman that unless she confessed,
her children would be picked up and turned over to a
county home. *Lynumn v. Illinois.*

● Mentally-dull 19-year-old was held incommunicado
for three days, was denied food for long periods, and
was told by the police chief that a mob was forming
outside to come and get him. *Payne v. Arkansas.*

● Lack of food, sleep or medication for high blood
pressure were factors where teams of several police
officers repeatedly questioned their prisoner until he
confessed. *Greenwald v. Wisconsin.*

● Police held the suspect incommunicado and questioned him continuously for 27 hours until he confessed. *US v. Murphy.*

● Officers allegedly told a wounded suspect at the
hospital he could not have water and would not be let
alone until he gave them the answers they wanted.
*Jackson v. Denno.*

- Police chief told a murder suspect that unless he confessed, his wife would be taken into custody. *Rogers v. Richmond.*

Courts have also found involuntariness resulting from intensive interrogation (especially if at night, using "tag teams" of fresh interrogators to wear down an exhausted suspect, or for prolonged periods without food or rest), as well as from implied promises to release codefendant-relatives, or to put the suspect into protective custody, or to obtain an OR release, or to arrange for psychiatric help.

**In fact, anytime an interrogator says anything to a suspect to imply that he will be better off in any way after confessing — except to clear his conscience — the interrogator is most likely rendering any subsequent statement involuntary and inadmissible.**

Few, if any, officers need to be reminded these days never to use or threaten unlawful force against a suspect. Not only would this sort of misconduct quickly turn a winning case into a sure loser in court, it would also create the potential for a civil rights lawsuit against the individual officer, his supervisors, and the jurisdiction employing him. Any officer on the losing side of such a lawsuit could lose his assets, his job, and his ability to get another one.

Many officers, however, inadvertently build due process problems into their interrogations because they simply don't realize that subtle psychological pressures, and even "playing the good guy" with favors for the "cooperative" suspect, can quickly make a statement just as legally inadmissible as if it had been extracted by torture. To avoid such problems, it's a good idea during your interrogations to **NEVER use such expressions as the following:**

"I'll see what I can do for you."

"We're going to do everything we can to help you."

"If it's a mental problem, maybe we can help you with this part of the treatment, or you know what might happen."

"You can do this the hard way, or the easy way."
"You're not leaving this room until I get the truth."

"The last guy that tried to bullshit me wound up on death row."

"We've got a jailhouse full of assorted perverts who would just love to get a fresh asshole like you in the showers tonight."

"Whoever did this thing is sick. He doesn't need any punishment — he just needs help."

Got the picture? These are the frustration tactics of an unskilled interrogator who has to resort to bribes and intimidation to produce statements because he hasn't mastered the art of interrogation. Whenever you hear an interrogator using this kind of language, you'll know two things immediately: the interrogator is not someone whose technique you'll want to waste your time studying, and you've just seen an officer grant testimonial immunity to a criminal suspect by turning everything the suspect says into involuntary, inadmissible, ruined evidence.

It's true that in each of the cases where the preceding language was used the interrogator eventually did obtain incriminating statements, but the convictions based on them — including one for multiple murder — were all reversed:

> Due process of law requires that statements obtained as these were cannot be used in any way against a defendant at his trial.
> *Mincey v. Arizona*

As noted several pages back, in order to insure that a suspect's statement has been given voluntarily, it's necessary not only to avoid undue influences which could overbear his free will, but also to consider any critical impairment to his capacity to choose to make a voluntary statement. If any police coercive influence has been used, a confession may be deemed involuntary if, at the time it was given, the suspect was so impaired as to lack the ability to exercise his free will in a rational manner (*Colorado v. Connelly*).

In *Fikes v. Alabama*, the Supreme Court ruled involuntary a confession taken from a mentally subnormal accused.

In *Townsend v. Sain*, a 19-year-old heroin addict described as a "near mental defective" was held incapable of giving a voluntary confession.

A 14-year-old questioned incommunicado for five days was found incapable of rational choice in *Gallegos v. Colorado*.

The defendant in *Jackson v. Denno* said he had been questioned while he lay wounded at hospital, "in pain and gasping for breath," shortly after drugs had been administered. The Supreme Court opined that "if Jackson's version

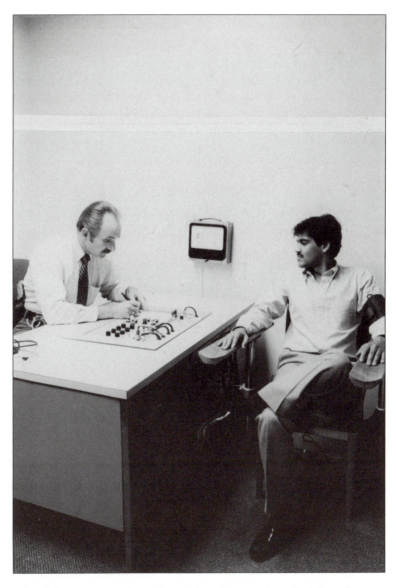

*The right to counsel can be violated, even though Miranda does not apply or has been waived.*

of the facts is accepted, the confession was involuntary and inadmissible."

In *Mincey v. Arizona*, the interrogation of Mincey in the hospital during his treatment for a gunshot wound, while "encumbered by tubes, needles and breathing apparatus," produced statements held not to be "the product of his free and rational choice."

In addition to traumatic injury, youthful age and low intelligence, other factors which might raise voluntariness issues include the influence of drugs or alcohol, lack of sleep, lack of food or water, shock, mental aberrations, emotional displays (anger, excitement, depression, fear) and religious or political fanaticism.

Whenever you encounter any condition, before or during your interrogation of a suspect, which might conceivably raise an issue of the suspect's capacity to confess voluntarily, take these three steps:

1) Identify and define the extent of the possible impairment. This may include questions of the suspect, a doctor's exam, inquiries of his friends or family, and running his rap.

2) Neutralize the incapacitating condition, if possible. Provide medical care, opportunity for sleep, food and water, and a chance for emotional outbursts to subside. (There's no point in exploiting these conditions to obtain a confession that's simply going to be thrown out on due process grounds. Be patient.) Adjust your vocabulary to the level of youthful and unintelligent suspects.

3) Before beginning substantive interrogation, ask the suspect to answer a series of questions designed to show that he was, in fact, capable of coherent conversation and rational judgments. For example, ask (and record his answers on tape or in writing) if he knows what time it is, what day of the week it is, the date, where he is, who you are, when/where/what he last ate, when he last slept, if he is injured, how he feels, if he's on medication or under a doctor's care, and what he thinks about police, or lawyers, or judges, or doctors, in general. Try to find out how far he went in school, what kinds of grades he made, which sports he participated in, what kinds of jobs he's had, what his hobbies are, whether he served in the military (branch, length, rank, type of discharge), etc.

These steps may seem tedious, but remember they're only necessary where the circumstances suggest an impaired-capacity/voluntariness issue, and unless you go to the trouble to establish the suspect's rational intellect, you may as well not bother going to the trouble to get a cop-out. Your patience and thoroughness in eliminating unwarranted defense opportunities to exclude the defendant's damaging admissions will be worth the extra effort!

**Recap:** For Fourteenth Amendment/due process purposes, the watchword is "voluntariness." When interrogating.

- Don't make promises.
- Don't make threats.
- Don't overlook impaired capacity.

## Chapter 11

# STRATEGY:
# YOUR OBJECTIVES

In spite of what some defense attorneys and judges seem to think, you're not just picking names out of the phone book and hauling people in for questioning. When you decide to interrogate someone, it's because you already know, or strongly suspect, that he committed the particular crime you're investigating. You're too busy and too conscientious to waste your time barking up the wrong tree.

So if the person you're interrogating has committed the crime, your objective is simply to get him to admit it, right? Wrong. It's not really that simple at all. As with everything else we've discussed, there's more to this part of your science than the casual television viewer realizes.

If you don't mind the analogy, the cops-and-robbers business is, in its way, a war — a military campaign. It's the good guys (you) against the bad guys (the crooks), and contrary to the way Hollywood dramatizes it in their fantasies, the real war on crime isn't won with blazing guns and brute force out on the street. The showdown, after all, takes place in the courtroom, where all that finally matters is which side had the superior strategy aimed at producing a favorable jury verdict. If the person you're interrogating committed a crime, your objective is to bring him to the justice of a verdict of "guilty." A simple admission won't do it.

To begin with, *admissions* are only intermediate objectives you have to take on your way to getting a *confession*. Although the words "admission" and "confession" are loosely used by the public at large as interchangeable terms, in the science of criminal investigation, they are distinct words with precise legal meanings:

- An "admission" is a statement that, by itself, does not acknowledge guilt of an offense but which tends to prove guilt when considered together with other evidence. For example, if your suspect says, "I was there when it happened," he has admitted his opportunity to have committed the crime, but he hasn't acknowledged guilt. If he says, "I hated his (decedent's) guts," he has admitted a motive to kill, but hasn't acknowledged guilt.

- A "confession," on the other hand, is a statement admitting participation in the crime and admitting every fact necessary to constitute an acknowledgment of guilt, including any specific intent, motive, guilty knowledge or other mental state required to establish guilt. For example, if a theft suspect tells you, "I knew that $100 bill belonged to my employer, but I took it without permission and I had no intention of ever paying it back," he has admitted every fact necessary to establish his guilt, in most jurisdictions.

Notice in the last example that if the theft statute in your jurisdiction contains all three elements (a taking of the personal property of another, without permission, and with the specific intent to permanently deprive the owner of possession), you would have only *admissions* — and not a *confession* — if the suspect had copped to any two of the elements but not to the third.

Now, since your suspect is not usually going to be a lawyer and isn't going to know or care about the nice distinctions between admissions and confessions or what all he has to admit in order to give you a full confession, *you* have to know what you need from him in order to get it. What do you need in every case?

You need the suspect's personal confirmation of each element of all three components of a criminal prosecution. Before any defendant can be convicted of any offense in any court in any jurisdiction, the prosecution must establish these three things:

1) Jurisdiction over the crime

2) Corpus of the crime

3) Identity of the perpetrator

The *jurisdictional* component has two elements: *time* and *place*. To prosecute a case, the state's attorney has to establish that the offense occurred within the applicable statute of limitations period. And before the court where the case is brought can render an enforceable judgment against the defendant, the attorney has to establish that sufficient criminal acts (though not necessarily all of them) took place within the court's geographical jurisdiction. During EVERY criminal interrogation you conduct, therefore, one of your intermediate objectives should be the suspect's acknowledgment of the time and place of his criminal participation. (As discussed further below, you should do this *regardless* of any other evidence of jurisdiction you have.)

The *corpus* of the crime, often referred to as the "elements," will be set out in the statute defining the crime. The corpus may consist of one or more acts occurring together, or committed in a certain way or by specified weapons, or while in a specified mental or physical state. Compare, for example, the statutory definitions in your jurisdiction of such crimes as murder, rape, receiving stolen property, driving under the influence, and possession of heroin for sale. You'll see that some require a specific intent, and some don't; some specify a level of intoxication; others require a certain knowledge or purpose.

Obviously, before you can interrogate a suspect about *any* offense, you have to know every element comprising the corpus; otherwise, you risk settling for *admissions* when you might have had a *confession*. And always remember that every element you neglect to nail down can (and probably will) be seized on by the crook's lawyer to form the basis of a defense in court.

For example, even experienced homicide investigators sometimes overlook the fact that it isn't sufficient simply to get an admission from the suspect that "I did it — I killed them." Killing, after all, may be either first or second degree murder (or third, in some states), or voluntary or involuntary manslaughter. Under some circumstances, it may not even be a crime at all (self-defense, accident, etc.).

The element that usually makes the difference in homicide cases is the perpetrator's *mental state*: was the killing intentional? Premeditated? With malice aforethought? Due to sudden anger? While under diminished capacity? Because of an irresistible impulse?

The thing about mental elements, whether malice or specific intent or guilty knowledge or other, is that there are two *and only two* ways to prove them — by circumstantial evidence, or by the suspect's admission. If an interrogator neglects to obtain an admission to the existence of the requisite mental element, the prosecutor is left to circumstantial evidence for proof, and it's well known what juries think of circumstantial evidence. So, cover *every* element.

If your statute on burglary, for example, defines the crime as entering a building with intent to steal, you don't have a *confession* if you settle for admissions from the suspect that he entered and then stole — he must admit that he *intended* to steal at the time of his entry (otherwise, you set up the defense of a trespass with a theft as an afterthought — less serious offenses than burglary).

If your statute on rape requires proof of penile penetration of the vagina, you can't settle for an admission that "I got on top of her and raped her." You want specific admissions to each and every element of the offense, including that his penis went inside her vagina. (Also see proof techniques in Chapter 14.)

When taking a statement from a cocaine dealer, you want admissions that the suspect knew the powder in the bindles and baggies was cocaine, that he knowingly possessed it, and that he intended to sell it. Etcetera.

You've got to know what you want before you can expect to get it. Be patient. Be methodical. Be thorough. And be greedy: don't settle for *admissions* when what you want — and what your prosecutor needs — is a *confession*.

The third component of a criminal lawsuit, *identity*, is the one that's difficult to overlook. In fact, some investigators become so preoccupied in their interrogations with getting the suspect to say, "I did it" — and so pleased with themselves when they succeed — that they forget to go back and have the suspect tell exactly what it was that he did, and when, and where, and why, and how, etc. Instead, all their police report states is that "the suspect admitted his involvement in the crime."

"The suspect admitted his involvement in the crime" is not a confession. It probably isn't even a legally admissible admission (subject to objection as vague and conclusionary). "The suspect admitted his involvement in the crime" is probably nothing more than a waste of eight words, and an indication of wasted time and lost opportunity during the interrogation, and another tell-tale sign of an unskilled interrogator.

Your primary objective, remember, is not merely to "break" the suspect during interrogation, but to obtain a legally admissible confession that will be of some use to your prosecutor in court in the effort to bring the criminal to justice. An interrogator who settles for "Okay, you got me, I did it" and reports that "the suspect admitted his involvement in the crime," hasn't given his prosecutor much ammunition for the big battle in court. (See reporting suggestions in Chapter 14.) While you've got your suspect talking, you want it all: jurisdiction, each and every element of the corpus, and ID.

And while you're at it, there's something else you want. Another legitimate objective of your interrogation is to *block the criminal's* avenues of retreat. Once he gets into court and has a lawyer appointed, and once the lawyer gets through telling him how stupid he was to waive his rights and start talking to you, the crook and his lawyer will start going through the statements you took, looking to see what rat holes you were careless enough to leave open. When they find a good one, they'll start plotting their strategy for slipping through it at trial.

Your objective, of course, is not to leave the guilty crook any loopholes. That means that after you've obtained complete admissions covering jurisdiction, corpus and ID, you should anticipate likely defenses to all of the possible charges and take appropriate disclaimers from the crook to negate them.

In a murder investigation, for example, negate self defense, diminished capacity, mistake, accident, defense of others, sudden quarrel, heat of passion, and any other legal grounds a defendant might have in your jurisdiction to reduce his culpability. In a rape case, take appropriate statements to negate a defense of consent; if the crime is assault, negate self defense; if the crime is offering to sell narcotics, negate the defense of entrapment; in DUI cases, negate the "chug-a-lug" defense; for NSF check charges, negate the possibility of checkbook miscalculations; negate the defense of necessity in auto theft cases, etc.

No list of charges and their typical defenses would be accurate for all jurisdictions; if you're assigned to work a particular detail, consult your local prosecutor or legal advisor to find out which defenses are available to defendants in your jurisdiction for the kinds of crimes you work, and then be sure to cover them during your interrogation.

There's no way for either you or your prosecutor to know exactly what evidence is going to be available in any case by the beginning of the trial, after the dust has settled from all the pretrial motions and other defense maneuvers. That's why you should investigate every case on the basis of two assumptions:

1) Assume that all of the witnesses and all other evidence in the case are going to be excluded or otherwise unavailable, and that whether the case is going to be won or lost will depend entirely on the *statements* you get from the crook: will you have an admissible confession, covering every element of jurisdiction, the corpus, and ID? Will the statement you take seal off every unwarranted defense theory the crook and his lawyer could have cooked up?

2) Assume that the suspect's statements will be ruled inadmissible (even if you've done everything correctly, it isn't impossible that the prosecutor or judge may make a mistake, or that the rules of evidence may change prior to trial). Never depend on the confession to prove the case — continue to investigate other sources of evidence and to work the case as though a guilty verdict is going to depend entirely on the *extrinsic evidence* of the suspect's commission of the crime.

In fact, in most jurisdictions, the rules of evidence require at least some slight evidence, independent of the defendant's confession, to corroborate the occurrence of the crime. This extrinsic evidence need not establish jurisdiction or ID, but must independently show the corpus of the crime before a suspect's confession to that crime can be admitted against him. This rule is intended to prevent the conviction of a compulsive confessor, or of a pressured or guilt-ridden individual, for a nonexistent crime.

For example, a distraught mother who feels guilty over her baby's crib death might confess to suffocating the baby; but unless there are bruises or marks or medical evidence to suggest the death was caused by human agency, the confession is inadmissible. Therefore, always seek extrinsic evidence of each element of the corpus, notwithstanding that you have a signed confession.

Here's a questionnaire for you. Do you handcuff every prisoner you transport, or only "dangerous" ones? Do you mug and print every arrestee you book into jail, or only some of them? Do you try to solve every case that's assigned to you, or only the most serious ones? Do you take careful notes in all of your investigations, or only for felonies? Do you expect the prosecutor to treat all of your arrests conscientiously, or only the most serious ones?

Last question: do you make an attempt to get a confession from *every* offender you arrest, or only from the most serious ones? This question has to be asked, unfortunately, because there seems to be an attitude, in some official quarters, that "interrogation" is something that only happens in cases of homicide, robbery, sexual assault and child molest, and sometimes only if ID is in issue.

Remember what Justice White said? "The defendant's own confession is probably the most probative and damaging evidence that can be admitted against him." If this is true (and it surely is), why would *any* officer, investigating *any* kind of offense, ever neglect an effort to collect this most probative and damaging evidence?

Does it make sense, for example, to collect pry mark evidence at the burglary scene and *not* interrogate the suspected burglar? Is it logical to analyze paint scrapings from a hit-and-run vehicle and *not* interrogate the suspected driver? Is there any good reason to preserve blood samples in a routine DUI arrest and *not* interrogate the driver?

In *every* case you present for indictment or complaint, your prosecutor needs the most probative and damaging evidence you can possibly develop. In *every* case, that

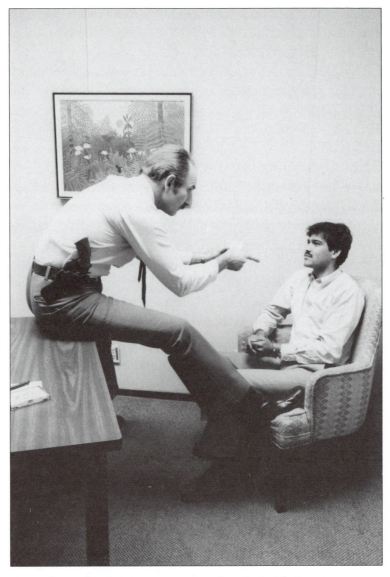

*Assuming a dominating posture and an intimidating manner only works well in the movies.*

evidence is the suspect's confession. Why limit the best available evidence to only the most serious offenses, and settle for lesser-quality evidence in other cases? Why give the bad guys that kind of tactical advantage in their battle strength?

"Interrogation" should not be something that only happens in homicides. It should be standard police work — indeed, it is the ultimate art of police work — in every criminal investigation you undertake, regardless of the charge, regardless of the extrinsic evidence, and even regardless of the fact that you yourself saw the perpetrator commit the crime. No investigation is complete unless interrogation has at least been *attempted*. It doesn't make sense to settle for less...does it?

Nothing in this chapter — or in the remainder of this book, for that matter — is intended to suggest that law enforcement officials have any legitimate interest in obtaining a confession from an innocent party, or of disabling a suspect of any defense which is properly available to him under the law. For the most part, law enforcement officers are dedicated men and women who have chosen their careers precisely because of their personal respect for the law, and it is paradoxical to reason that they would be motivated to compromise their standards and their chances of apprehending the truly guilty by purposely misdirecting their efforts toward an innocent suspect.

Innocence can usually be very quickly and easily demonstrated; *guilt* requires patient, careful and methodical uncovering. The general approaches and particular tactics suggested in this chapter and the several chapters following are intended to help increase police proficiency at the expense of the guilty and without risk to the innocent, recognizing that the ultimate objective is justice.

(Although some people disagree, a legitimate objective of interrogation in some circumstances is simply to solve unsolved cases — to "clear paper." If all of the circumstances of a case convince you that you will never have any realistic prospect of obtaining any legally admissible statements, but that you probably *can* get *inadmissible* statements from a suspect by noncoercive means, an interrogation "outside *Miranda*" or subject to some other constitutional objection in court may still be useful to clear cases. Caution: don't be too quick to throw in the towel on admissibility issues. It's best to check with the prosecutor before deciding to seek an inadmissible statement just to clear paper.)

*Chapter 12*

# STRATEGY: SUSPECT EVALUATION

Will you use exactly the same interrogation tactics on every suspect you interrogate, in every case? Of course not. What works on one person may not work on another.

What is it that determines which particular tactics you choose? Partly, it's the nature and circumstances of the crime. It's also how much you already know and how much extrinsic evidence you have. To some extent, its your individual personality and experience. But more than anything else, it's your evaluation of the particular suspect you're dealing with.

This important step for the criminal investigator is analogous to the military strategist gathering and analyzing intelligence on his enemy, or the football coach studying scouting reports and play-action footage on the opposing team: if you don't know and understand what strengths, weaknesses and objectives your adversary has, you can't plot your strategy for succeeding with him. Without a strategy, you're likely just to try to repeat whatever happened to have worked for you last. That's nothing more than trial and error;

trial and error as a substitute for intelligent strategy has such a low ratio of success that most professionals wouldn't dare depend on it — not the general, not the coach, not the trial lawyer, not the scientist. Why should you?

You shouldn't. And you don't have to. Most of the intelligence you need on your subject you've been accumulating and processing all your life, and especially since you become a law enforcement officer. That's because your subject has many behavioral patterns in common with everyone else, and you've been digesting information about human behavior ever since you were a baby and learned how to act to produce a desired response from others. In the course of your police work, you've become especially aware of the particular behavioral traits of people who have done something wrong and are trying to conceal it.

So both consciously and unconsciously, you've been amassing and analyzing intelligence data that will form the basis of your suspect evaluation. You may not have stopped to think about what you've learned in these terms, but if you do, you'll realize that you were already aware of the following attributes of your suspect:

● He is experiencing some degree of *fear*.

● He may or may not be feeling *shame* or *guilt* about having committed the crime.

● Whether or not he *regrets* having committed the crime, he regrets at least some parts of his conduct — those "stupid things" he did that allowed him to get caught; therefore, he's experiencing some degree of *self-blame or self criticism*.

- Since he probably hadn't expected to be identified and/or caught by the police — and now he has been — he has to be experiencing some degree of *self-doubt* about his judgment of how clever he is and how stupid the cops are. He's quickly trying to recalculate his degree of superiority over victims, witnesses and police officers who have somehow gotten the upper hand.

- If the opinions of his friends, family and co-workers matter to him, he is experiencing feelings of *embarrassment* or humiliation that they already know, or will soon find out, about his arrest.

- Unless he has been arrested before, he will probably be operating under misconceptions about crime and punishment learned from television and the movies, and he'll have a considerable amount of *uncertainty* about what's going to happen to him next, and eventually.

- If he's had little experience at handling trauma and crisis in his life (and to a lesser extent if he's more experienced), he will be *impatient* for some kind of resolution to his predicament.

- Seeing himself as the center of attention, he could have an unaccustomed feeling of *importance*.

- Any moral or religious convictions he may have would generate some sense of a need for *expiation and absolution*.

- Falling back on his customary habits for avoiding uncomfortable consequences, if he normally tries to escape by running, he will be experiencing the *frustration* of the caged animal; if he normally defends himself by fighting, he'll be feeling *hostility*; if he usually tries to talk his way out of things, he may have a *compulsion to talk*; if he usually just gives up and hopes for mercy or luck to save him, he should be feeling *submissiveness*. (One of these attitudes will normally become quite obvious to you at your initial contact with the suspect, before interrogation ever begins. When he betrays his defensive posture, of course, he tips you off to the best tactics to use against him.)

- Most people being naturally motivated to see things in the best possible light for themselves (even unrealistically so), he may be hopefully concentrating on all the ways things could go his way, giving him some *optimism*.

- Caught in unfamiliar surroundings without his usual base of support, and facing some perceived prospect of unfavorable consequences, he will almost certainly be experiencing a strong sense of *insecurity*.

- Seeing you as the immediate threat to his chances of extricating himself from his plight, and therefore needing to size you up as an adversary (the same thing you're doing with him), he'll be somewhat under the influence of his *curiosity* about you.

*Your evaluation of the suspect as an adversary should be far more accurate than his evaluation of you.*

There are countless other physiological and psychological factors shaping his defensive posture, of course. But without needing to catalogue all of them, you already know *in general* that the combination of emotions the suspect has to contend with before and during a police interrogation splits his attention in so many directions, and preoccupies him so substantially, that concentration on his defensive strategy can't receive the attention he might wish to give it. That means that in most cases, there is a built-in opportunity for a properly-conducted interrogation to succeed at eliciting the truth out of the suspect's mouth.

But don't rely solely on this kind of "standard intelligence" about how apprehended criminals can be expected to behave, *in general*. You also want, whenever possible and from whatever sources are available, to gather as much *special* intelligence as you can on your individual suspect. To complete your suspect evaluation, try to find out the following (*before* interrogation, if possible; *during* interrogation, if necessary), as appropriate to the case (this step may be vital in a homicide interrogation and unwarranted in a petty larceny interrogation):

— Suspect's age
— Family status
— Occupation
— Education
— Military experience
— Birthplace/hometown
— Financial situation
— Physical/medical condition
— Hobbies/interests
— Prior police record/standard MO
— Probation/parole status
— Personality traits

Sources for this kind of special intelligence on your suspect may include his family members, friends, employer, co-workers, neighbors, accomplices, victims, witnesses, arresting officers, booking officers, custodial officers, suspect's wallet and other items found on him at booking, official records, and, of course, the suspect himself.

The final category of intelligence you ought to have before beginning interrogation, if possible, is complete information about the circumstances of the crime, including evidence of the suspect's motive, opportunity, means and participation, and details of his apprehension and pre- interrogation confinement. You need to analyze this category of information to determine what is *known*, what is *suspected* as probable, and what is completely *unknown* about the suspect's crime. (This determination will be significant in your interrogation sequence, as discussed in the next chapter.) The circumstances of the case will not only affect your suspect evaluation but will also help identify the potential defenses your interrogation will need to cover.

Once you know your objectives and your suspect, you're ready to consider what kinds of tactics are most likely to allow you to achieve your objectives, given the strength of the opposition you may encounter from your adversary.

*Chapter 13*

# STRATEGY:
# YOUR TACTICS

Here's an easy exercise in basic logic. Again, these are things that you already know, but may never have consciously analyzed in this manner. Let's consider some possibilities.

In any criminal investigation where you get access to the suspect for a potential interrogation opportunity, there are two possibilities: you're going to achieve your objective of an admissible confession, *or* you're not. Arithmetically, you have one chance out of two, depending on some further possibilities.

After you've recited or read the *Miranda* warning to the suspect, there are two possibilities: he may choose to invoke his rights and not discuss the case, *or* he may choose to waive and talk. One chance in two.

If he invokes, of course, there isn't going to be any confession. If he decides to waive his rights and talk to you, there are two possibilities: he may decide to tell you the truth about his participation in the crime, *or* he may decide to lie. One chance in two.

If he decides to tell the truth, all you have to do in taking his confession is to be thorough in covering capacity, voluntariness, jurisdiction, corpus, ID and potential defenses, and to preserve suitable proof (see Chapter 14).

If the suspect decides to lie about his commission of the crime, there are two possibilities: he will accurately evaluate his situation and his adversary (you) and adopt a defensive posture and tactics which are well-suited to preventing successful interrogation, *or* he will miscalculate the relative strengths and weaknesses and pursue defensive tactics which, based on false assumptions, practically guarantee the success of your skillful interrogation.

Therefore, out of all of the possibilities which involve the suspect's choices, only two of them represent obstacles in the path of your objective: his decision not to waive *Miranda*, and his decision to be deceitful in accordance with his accurate view of his situation and best defenses.

Conversely, your job of helping to secure criminal justice is made easier if the suspect chooses to waive his rights, and then chooses either to tell you the truth or to deceive you with ineffective tactics. Therefore, to the extent that you can lawfully and properly do so, you want to employ tactics which are conductive to the suspect's decisions to follow these latter courses, and avoid practices which might prompt him to invoke *Miranda* or to correctly calculate and defend.

All pretty obvious and elementary so far, right? Next, notice that except for those crooks who have been through the mill so often with so many lawyers that they've finally been conditioned never to waive and never to talk, a suspect's decision about whether to waive or invoke actually depends on how he has already decided to choose among the remaining possibilities. That is to say, even though waiver-or-invocation is chronologically the first set of choices you present to him, the other choices have to be made first in his mind before he can decide between invoking and waiving.

Unless he's a dysfunctional human being, he's going to do whatever he perceives to be in his best interest. If he evaluates his situation and sizes up his adversary and decides he can do himself the most good by not talking about what he did, he'll invoke. If he decides that he can improve his situation and obtain some relief by *either* telling you the truth or deceiving you into believing that he's innocent, it's in his self interest to talk, and so he'll waive.

Since you want him to talk, you want him to perceive his predicament and his adversary (you) in such a way that he will conclude *either* that you can be trusted, or that you can be fooled. Now, notice (put yourself in his shoes if it helps to visualize) that the kind of adversary who satisfies *both* of these possibilities is a quiet, kindly, non-threatening, patient, sincere, understanding, friendly and not-too-bright police officer, whose manner seems to suggest that this investigation isn't really any big deal.

To put it another way, if you were the crook, knowing you were guilty and had been caught dirty, trying to cope with the insecurity and emotional conflict of your situation and hoping to find some way to get relief, would you feel more comfortable talking to someone with all the characteristics of the "friendly bungler" described above, or being interrogated by a belligerent, intimidating, unsympathetic, macho cop who lets you know up front how clever he is, and whose attitude tells you your neck is already in the noose and he's going to tighten the rope as soon as he scares a confession out of you? In the real world, who would be more likely to get a waiver and a cop-out — Columbo or Dirty Harry?

The *Miranda* decision says you can't "threaten, trick or cajole" the suspect into waiving his rights, but nothing says you can't outsmart him. In order to get a waiver, you can't tell the suspect a lie about how much peril he's facing, but nothing says you have to reveal everything you know about how deep his trouble really is, or how much proof of his guilt you already have, or how critical his confession may be to you:

> Events occurring outside of the presence of the suspect and entirely unknown to him surely can have no bearing on the capacity to comprehend and knowingly relinquish a constitutional right...we have never read the Constitution to require that the police supply a suspect with a flow of information to help him calibrate his self interest in deciding whether to speak or stand by his rights.
> *Moran v. Burbine*

Although *Miranda* requires you to caution the custodial suspect that his statements will be used against him in court, nothing requires you to warn him that you are more expert at spotting lies than he is at telling them, or that even his attempts to deceive you may provide just the proof the prosecutor will need of a consciousness of guilt:

> This Court has never embraced the theory that a defendant's ignorance of the full consequences of his decisions vitiates their voluntariness.... Thus, we have not held that the sine qua non for a knowing and voluntary waiver of the right to remain silent is a full

and complete appreciation of all of the consequences flowing from the nature and the
quality of the evidence in the case.

*Oregon v. Elstad*

And although due process considerations prohibit telling the suspect that all you really want to do is to help him out
of trouble, nothing prohibits your behaving in a friendly,
civil, humane manner toward him. And nothing says that you
may not permit a suspect the conceit of overestimating his
own presence of mind and underestimating yours:

...the state of mind of the police is irrelevant to the question of the intelligence and
voluntariness of respondent's election to abandon his rights.

*Moran v. Burbine*

There is, therefore, nothing unlawful or improper in
neutralizing your adversary's apprehension about the level
of threat you represent to him, nor in choosing not to reveal
the true extent of your intelligence. A suspect who sizes you
up as a menacing or clever adversary is not likely to conclude
that his self interest will be best served by talking to you; it's
in *your* self interest, therefore, not to come on like Dirty
Harry, but to permit the suspect to feel comfortable about
being able to tell you the truth, or to feel confident about
being able to tell you a lie. Either way, he waives; and either
way, you're on the road to a confession.

This is not to suggest that you have to put on some
complicated, contrived act of being an all-forgiving incom-
petent. But if you've been in the law enforcement profession
very long, you know that this advice (that you take every

lawful step to lower the suspect's level of alarm and to allow him to underestimate you) is contrary to the technique recommended in some other publications. And if you've watched three or more different officers conduct interrogations, the odds are you saw at least one of them employ a "tough guy" technique. That may work in a small percentage of cases, where the suspect was already predisposed to confess, but logic and experience and human nature tell us you'll enjoy a much higher rate of success with tactics designed to outsmart, rather than to intimidate, the suspect.

Note though that this "friendly bungler" approach is not really the same thing as the trite notion of "establishing rapport with the suspect." Although the word "rapport" is often used in discussing interrogation techniques, the idea that a police officer ever actually establishes any rapport with a crook he's investigating is paradoxical, if not sometimes disgusting. Look it up — "rapport" is a close relationship marked by mutual feelings and harmony. That's not what's going on in your interrogation at all.

The individual you're interrogating has driven his car in a dangerous manner, or he stole, or robbed, or assaulted, or molested, or raped, or killed! You've dedicated your career — and on occasion risked your life — to apprehend such criminals and to do everything you lawfully can to see that they're punished! Close relationship? Mutual feelings? Harmony? Not likely. Rapport? Not really.

What you're doing isn't called "rapport." Letting the crook fool himself into relative vulnerability is called "tactical superiority." What you're patiently and wisely doing is called the art of interrogation.

Once you accept the wisdom of getting waivers and confessions by tactics which *disarm* rather than *alert* the suspect, a number of practices consistent with your strategy become fairly obvious:

- If you give the *Miranda* warning at a time when the suspect's alert level is high, he's less likely to waive. Moreover, no warning is necessary until you're ready to begin custodial questioning. As a general policy, arresting officers should **not** *Mirandize* unless they intend to interrogate immediately. Until the suspect has had an opportunity to evaluate his predicament and conclude that discussions offer hope of relief, he has no incentive to waive. Don't rush the warning.

- Likewise, don't *Mirandize* while the suspect is in a cell or cage, or is handcuffed, or is recovering from police-inflicted injuries sustained in the arrest, or is surrounded by uniformed or gun-toting officers. Reduce his perceptions that he's in a hostile environment which requires high levels of caution.

- Eliminate symbols of officialdom — no stenographers, no open case files, no "witnesses," no badges, no guns, no police radios, no isolation "interrogation rooms" (security permitting). The less official, less formal and less serious the suspect views his treatment, the more likely he'll waive and talk openly.

- Show concern for the suspect's welfare. Ask if he needs a drink of water or coffee, or to go to the restroom. Don't overdo this to the point of the "clever softening up" routine disapproved by the courts (see Chapter 8). If he was injured during the crime or apprehension, ask if he's satisfied with the medical treatment he's had, and how he's feeling (necessary for due process reasons).

- Don't outnumber the suspect. If he sees that there's only one of him against two or three police officers, his survival instincts will automatically heighten, and you reduce your prospects of getting a waiver. If your session is not being recorded, you want a witness to his waiver and statements, of course. But put the witness out of sight, or behind the two-way mirror, or at the other end of the bug. In your office or other interview room, you want the informality, the privacy and the low-alert atmosphere of a one-on-one chat.

- Eliminate distractions. You don't want the phone to ring or another officer to barge through your door just as the suspect is about to give you a waiver or a critical answer during interrogation. You also don't want the suspect to look around the room and see Clint Eastwood posters or hangman's nooses or any of the other law-and-order symbols police officers use to decorate their offices.

- Don't sit behind a desk with the suspect facing you in the traditional interviewer-interviewee positions. Come out from behind the desk, pull up the same kind of chair the suspect has, and sit just a safe distance away, in a relaxed posture. Don't be exhibiting either a gun *or* an empty holster. If you're in uniform, stash your Sam Browne securely out of sight. If you're in a suit, hang up your coat and loosen or remove your tie. Don't look or act official or superior.

- Introduce yourself as simply as you can, including your first name; this is no time to be throwing the weight of all your impressive titles around; de-emphasize your own importance. As you introduce yourself, put you and the suspect on a first-name basis — and stay there. Compare: "Mr. Moreno, I'm Detective Sergeant Vasil of the Robber-Homicide Bureau" (too official too important, too clever, too threatening); "Hi, Mr. Moreno, I'm Officer Vince Vasil. Everybody calls me Vince, okay? Is it all right if I call you Danny, or do you go by Dan?"

- Your tone of voice, facial expressions and body language should convey the impression that you're an easy person to get along with, and to talk to. Don't use a somber, stiff, official tone of voice while explaining the suspect's rights. A cordial, pleasant tone of voice works better. Remember, you want your demeanor to say to the suspect, "I'm here to listen to your story," **not** "Watch out! Better not let your guard down with me!"

- There are at least three good reasons to read *Miranda* rights from a pre-approved card, even though you know it all from memory. For one thing, it helps insure that you always give an adequate warning and don't inadvertently omit something. For another, it makes proof easier: you can refer to the card while testifying, if necessary. And the tactical reason is that it may appear to the suspect that you're too simple-minded to memorize something that every Hill Street Blues fan knows by heart. Let him draw whatever conclusions he will.

Compare: "Mr. Moreno, it's my duty to warn you of your rights. You have the absolute right to remain silent..." (too alarming); "Danny, the first thing I need to do, if you'll bear with me just for a minute, I want to go through your rights with you and make sure you don't have any questions about them, and what I'd like to do, if you don't mind, is to just take them nice and slow, one at a time, and if you have any questions, we can stop and clarify what they mean, and the first thing is, let me just read it the way they have it written down here, is that you have the right to remain silent, and do you understand that okay?" Etc. This "run-on sentence" doesn't invite any responses from the suspect until it gets him down to the question mark. You don't particularly want to provoke interruptions from him until he's heard the whole pitch.

- An interrogation is no place to be a show-off with your impressive college vocabulary. Adjust your vocabulary to the suspect's level. Use plain talk (no police "gobbledygook" expressions!); use short words and simple phrases — some people don't understand words like "penile penetration" or "ejaculation" or "cognizant of the fact." **Keep it simple**!

- As you work your way through the four parts of the *Miranda* advisement, ask *after each part* if he understands it. If you wait until you've read all four parts and then ask, and if he says "No," you have to go back and find out which part or parts he didn't understand. Plus, throwing all four parts in and then asking for a "Yes" may make it seem like too much to swallow. It's better to feed him bite-size pieces that are easier to digest.

● After he has heard and understands all of the advisement, how do you phrase your waiver question? A fairly common formulation is, "Having each of these rights in mind, do you now wish to give up your rights and answer questions?" Not only is this kind of language not mandated by Supreme Court decisions, it also isn't mandated by good tactics.

If he's just confirmed, one by one, that he understands what his various rights are, there's no need to exhort him to "keep each of these rights in mind" as he decides what to do. And it's also unnecessary to phrase the waiver in terms of his "giving up rights" (emotional words of surrender), in order to "answer questions" (a one-sided grilling).

Tactically better, and perfectly legal under US Supreme Court decisions: "Okay, Danny, now that you understand your rights, then can we go ahead and talk about the case: Would that be all right with you, Danny?"

● Once you've tendered the waiver question, the suspect is ordinarily going to respond in one of three ways: he's going to invoke, he's going to waive, or he's going to ask you for some kind of explanation about consequences. There's a proper way to handle all three responses.

If he invokes, *stay with your strategy*. Remember that even though you now have to "scrupulously honor" his invocation and ask no questions, the suspect is probably remaining in custody, at least temporarily, and can always change his mind and re-initiate interrogation. Don't forget that in *Oregon v. Mathiason*, all it took was the suspect's question, "What's going to happen to me now?" So don't betray your strategy when the suspect tells you he doesn't want to talk — don't get angry, don't act indignant, and don't resort to intimidation. If you change your approach, you'll simply confirm to the suspect that he made the right choice in invoking. Since there's always a chance of his reopening discussions, it's better for him to be left with the feeling that all he's doing is denying himself an opportunity to talk.

If he doesn't invoke but asks you to explain consequences, *stay with your strategy*. Be interested in his concerns, no matter how stupid or trivial they may seem to be, and be careful not to create 14th Amendment voluntariness problems by implying that the consequences depend on his cooperation. Explain that you can't tell him about possible sentences, because that would be up to the judge. Do not misrepresent the law or the facts of the case at this stage. Do not be over-eager to obtain the waiver. Remain patient and friendly. If he decides to invoke after you've answered his questions, conduct yourself as above.

If he decides at either point to waive and talk to you, *stay with your strategy*. Don't immediately become officious and stick a written waiver form under his nose. Remember, he can decide at any time to exercise his rights and cut off further questioning. If you suddenly become more formal, more relieved or more clever, he may sense that he underestimated you, and may then invoke, or at least upgrade his defenses. If you want his signature on a written waiver form (and if you don't have a tape or an independent witness, you do), wait until much later, when he's irrevocably committed.

● Once you have your valid waiver, what's your next step? Many police reports describe the next occurrence this way: "After the suspect waived, I invited him to tell me about his involvement in the crime."

This sort of statement suggests that the officer isn't so much a skilled interrogator as a passive listener. Interrogation, remember, is *controlled* questioning; leaning back and allowing the suspect to say whatever he wants to, in his own words, is neither "questioning" nor "controlled." Any unskilled layman could sit there and be a passive listener. In fact, the officer could turn on a tape recorder and leave the room, with the same effect.

The crook doesn't know the elements of the crime — you do. He doesn't have any particular interest in covering jurisdiction, corpus, ID and defenses — you do. He doesn't know what you can already prove and what blanks you need him to fill in — you do. So he doesn't have any business controlling the direction or content of the interrogation. You do.

● One standard theory of interrogation is that you let the suspect tell you whatever phony version of the crime he pleases, and then you destroy his story, piece by piece, by pointing out inconsistencies and confronting him with known facts you're in a position to prove, or even with physical evidence. This technique is said to convince the suspect that it's useless trying to lie to you, and he will then confess.

Not likely. It's not easy for someone to sit and lie to you, making a psychological commitment to the truth of his story, and then turn around and admit that everything he just said was a lie. If you allow the suspect to commit to a lie, it's going to be that much harder for him to recant later and tell you the truth. What's more, if you show him that you're capable of tricking him that way, he becomes wary of everything else you say and do, and adjusts his defensive tactics to meet your cleverness, making it harder for you to trick him again. Or worse, he'll get angry at you, then angry at himself, and he'll say, "I think I need a lawyer." Is that what your want to hear?

It's better for you to *control your interrogation* from start to finish and try to keep him honest as you go along. If you can get it, what you'd prefer from the suspect is the truth. A refutable lie is a distant second choice.

● The first thing you want to do after you get a waiver, in staying with your strategy, is to reinforce the suspect's still-tentative decision that he can talk to you without the world caving in on him. You want to establish a pattern in which you ask a question, he gives you a truthful answer, you don't make any big deal of it, and he sees that he doesn't immediately suffer any harmful consequences. What you want to do is to condition him to telling you the truth, without fear or hesitation.

How can you do this? Start with easy, neutral things that don't have anything to do with the case and that he doesn't have any need to lie about. These may usually be the kinds of questions you need to ask anyway, to complete your profile for suspect evaluation. (It's highly unlikely any suspect would realize that you're serving these two purposes with apparently-innocuous questions.) Progress from having him confirm things you know, to having him tell you things you don't know.

For example: "Now, Danny, we're going to have plenty of time to talk about whatever we want to — there's not any hurry — and I want you to know that I'll listen to anything you want to say, and we can discuss things back and forth, if you want to — I'm going to leave that up to you. But could we just spend a few minutes here getting a little bit better acquainted? Because, see, I'd like to know more about you, and understand where you're coming from, and every-thing. I mean, really all I know is, I guess you live over on Logan Street, is that right?" Etc.

● As you listen to his answers and volunteered comments about his background, work and personal life, update your suspect evaluation, with an eye toward selecting the best approach for totally disarming his defenses against the truth. Consider these four possibilities:

1) *Lost cause.* Sometimes a defender can be induced to "throw in the towel" when he becomes convinced he can't possibly win, or that the cost of winning is too high. If you have a relatively strong case against a suspect in a relatively minor crime, he's more likely to capitulate than if he realizes you have a weak case against him on a serious charge. Considering your suspect evaluation, the nature of the charge and the quantum of extrinsic evidence, you may decide that a "show of force" (confronting him with the proof of his

guilt) will prompt him to confess the truth and hope for mercy. If so, stay with your strategy:

"Now, Danny, before we talk about why you did what you did, I want to be up-front with you and tell you what we have — and it looks to me like we have just about everything. I know you might have something to say about some of these things, but let me just lay it all out for you here first, and then we'll see where we stand on everything, all right? The first witness, Mr. Gaylord, saw...." (Never tell your suspect that a witness *says* he saw — be positive.)

Save the most incriminating piece of evidence for last, and after you've finished recounting everything, don't give him any chance to commit to a denial. Act as if his guilt is a foregone conclusion, and instead of asking him *if* he did the crime, frame your questions as if you're really only interested in clearing up minor details about *why* he did it, or *how* he did it, etc. Obviously, he can't say, "I did it because..." or "I did it like this," without implicitly or expressly saying, "I did it."

2) *Cat out of the bag.* No one is going to bother defending an objective that he believes is already in his adversary's hands, just as no one has any reason to continue to keep a confidence once he believes the secret is out. As suggested above, convincing the suspect that you already know the information you're actually seeking will probably remove his incentive for deception. If you already know he did it, he has no secret left to conceal.

In addition to confronting him with genuine evidence of his guilt, you can fabricate the existence of other evidence which would be plausible for him to believe you have, and test his reaction to it. Contrast this situation *after Miranda waiver* with the situation *before waiver*: you cannot lawfully "trick" the suspect into waiving his rights, because he has a constitutional right to remain silent, and constitutional rights can only be relinquished voluntarily. However, if he decides to waive his rights and speak, he has no constitutional right to lie. Therefore, the rule on use of tricks, ruse or deception is that you cannot use them to obtain a waiver, but *after waiver* you can use them to obtain a confession, provided they would not be likely to provoke an involuntary (and therefore unreliable) confession.

For example, in *Frazier v. Cupp*, officers falsely advised the suspect that his codefendant had given a confession implicating him; the suspect subsequently confessed, and the Supreme Court held that this misrepresentation by police did not make the confession involuntary or inadmissible.

Similarly, in *Oregon v. Mathiason*, the Supreme Court did not condemn the use by police of a false statement to the suspect about having discovered his fingerprints at the scene of the burglary. State court decisions have allowed such post-waiver deceptions as falsely telling a suspect he had been identified by an eyewitness, or that his gunshot residue test was positive, or that his minor injuries were actually very serious, or that he had dropped his wallet at the crime scene. Confessions obtained following these deceptions were held admissible.

Some suspects, of course, will respond to a bluff; others will call it, and challenge you to produce your claimed evidence. Leave yourself a way out (it's in the lab or the evidence locker or at the DA's office, or against department policy). Also, if you have two or more suspects in custody, interrogate the weakest one first; he'll be more susceptible to the bluff, and once you tape his cop-out, you can use it to show the tougher suspect that the cat is out of the bag.

3) *Diversion.* A defender can be fooled into pulling his defenses away from the actual objective if his adversary creates a diversion by giving the false impression that a decoy is the real objective. Your suspect may be inclined to open up about the crime he committed if he believes that you're trying to use him to get to someone else, or if the believes that you're primarily interested in connecting him to another crime that he can prove he didn't commit.

So if you have a crime committed by two or more crooks, or if you just want the suspect to think that you believe someone else was in on it with him to give him a scapegoat, you can act uninterested in what your suspect's role was. Again, take the position that you already know the suspect's part in the crime — that isn't even an open question. The only question is, what can he tell you about the *real* bad guy, his accomplice? ("How could your friend get away and leave you holding the bag, Danny? Why did you let him take all the risks while you got the easy part?" or vice versa; "This thing here was penny-ante compared to the one you did last year down in Britt City — was that one a lot harder to pull off?")

4) *Rationalization.* Even crooks have an innate sense of justice. If they can somehow rationalize their criminal conduct so that they can justify it to themselves and they have nothing to apologize for, it's easier for them to accept responsibility and admit to their acts than if they've offended not only society's sense of justice but their own, as well. So, for example, a man who believes that his shooting of another was justified by self-defense will be likely to admit to the act of shooting, whereas if he knows he can't even justify it to himself, he'll be more likely to deny it altogether.

You can't afford to defeat your own purpose. It doesn't do you any good to get a guilty crook to confess if you can only do so by suggesting a justification for his crime that amounts to a legal defense. So it wouldn't do for you to get the suspect to admit he shot the victim because the victim started the fight and was coming at him with a knife, unless you know you're in a position to completely disprove the suggested rationalization.

A safer technique is to appeal to a rationalization basis that, even if true, does not amount to a defense to the crime, or does not reduce the degree (the suspect may even mistakenly believe that a particular rationalization theory *is* a legal defense). For example, many people seek to rationalize their misconduct on the ground that *everybody else does it* ("Everyone cheats on their taxes, so why shouldn't I?"). When you're investigating the kind of crime that's commonly committed by "nice people," including shoplifting, NSF checks, drunk driving, possession of cocaine/marijuana, prostitution and other "status offenses," the suspect's ability to satisfy his innate sense of justice on this basis may lead him to conclude he has nothing to defend.

Another standard rationalization theory is that whatever happened was *earned* by the victim and/or the suspect ("I cut him up a little because he had it coming to him; I took my boss's money because I deserved it").

Some people can rationalize misbehavior with the excuse that the urge to do it was so great, they had *no ability to resist* ("I saw that necklace and I just *had* to have it!").

A related rationalization is that *need* makes right, or excuses wrong. Distinguish the legal defense of *necessity*, which would excuse some conduct in an emergency, such as having to run a red light to get an injured child to the hospital. The rationalization theory of *need* which falls short of defensible necessity is exemplified in the paperhanger's statement, "The only reason I wrote that check was because I needed the money to get my car fixed so I could get to my job."

There's also a mixture of *macho* pride and rugged individualism that produces a "go for it" recklessness about some kinds of criminal behavior — particularly where gang rivalries or personal honor may be seen to be at stake, as in vindictive assaults and killings ("Hey, man, ain't nobody gonna mess with my woman and stay out of the hospital").

And there's an *innate sense of fairness* which will permit the suspect to accept getting caught for the crime he actually committed, but makes him protest charges that he knows are unwarranted; even though it makes no difference in his *legal* guilt, an inflated charge offends his sense of *moral* guilt, and may

*"I'm sure we'd all love to believe you, officer, but where is your proof...hmmm?"*

prompt him to claim his actual degree of guilt just to set the record straight.

For example, you suspect the man you're interrogating of a residential burglary in which a camera and some cheap costume jewelry were taken. But you accuse your suspect of having taken expensive electronics gear, a gold coin collection, guns and expensive fine jewelry worth thousands of dollars, telling him, "It's all listed right here in the insurance claim the lady filed, Danny. How about it?"

His sense of outrage that he's getting blamed for more that he did — and that his "victim" is about to profit big from his crime and remain free while he goes to jail — may motivate him to set you straight about what he really stole. Since his burglary charge doesn't depend on the actual value stolen, his rationalization isn't any legal defense to anything.

To exploit these and any other rationalization theories you're able to identify, try to use questions instead of suggestions to channelize the suspect's thinking, and let the rationalization be *his* idea. This might prevent your appearing to a sympathetic jury to have been condoning the suspect's misconduct and giving them an excuse to do likewise. Be careful to avoid unwittingly laying the groundwork for a legal defense.

● Throughout your interrogation, avoid letting the suspect figure out your objective. Scatter the questions on the critical bits of information you need, in random order, among a greater number of irrelevant inquiries. Appear to be more interested in the irrelevant, harmless questions and their neutral answers than in the legally significant points. Don't proceed chronologically; jump around.

- Controlling your interrogation does not mean you should do all the talking. *Your* words aren't evidence. You should talk just enough to direct and draw out the suspect, and then let him talk about the details. His narrative accounts of things are far better than his simply saying "yes" or "no" to your leading questions.

- Keep the focus sharp. Only ask one thing at a time. No compound questions.

- Don't say to the suspect, "I tend to believe you." After you do, you can't very well ask him to change his story.

- Don't ask, "Can you remember...?" That gives the suspect an easy way to evade answering. Don't accept that he can't remember anything. Ask for his best recollection.

- Call the suspect by his first name frequently.

- The first time you go through the details of the crime with him, avoid legal terms and emotional words such as "rape, beat, strangle, molest, steal," etc. Just talk about what he physically did in the most neutral language you can use: "The things you took...the woman you screwed...the little girl you touched...how you got the best of him..." etc. After the suspect has made all the necessary *factual* admissions, you can unceremoniously substitute specific *legal* terms the next time through his statement, so that he has finally admitted both that he "touched" the little girl and that he "molested" her.

● If the suspect persists in a denial of the crime, marry him to details that can be disproven at trial. Ask him plenty of "how?" and "why?" questions that force him to commit to a hastily-contrived story that can be used at trial to prove his consciousness of guilt. Jump back and forth, out of logical order.

● Don't be easy to satisfy. Don't let the suspect deflect your interrogation from your objective by giving you part of what you want. Whenever he makes a partial admission, stay with your strategy. Act as if you already knew what he just told you, which isn't really any big deal, but what about...?

And even after you get a full confession and all of the statements you need for the case under investigation, stay greedy: "Now that you're getting honest with me, Danny, and you're getting this off your chest and cleaning your conscience, I know there's a few other things you've done that you want to clean up now that you're straightening out your act. Which one do you want to talk about first?" (Even if you can't possibly prosecute, you may as well clear paper.) Also, see if he wants to finger other criminals.

● Tie the suspect into the physical evidence and the crime scene. Have him describe where the scene is and how to get to it, so there's no question later that he was copping-out to the same crime you were investigating. Have him ID the evidence and describe how it fits into the picture. As appropriate, have him date and sign or initial each item of evidence that he confirms.

● If there is property, a body or evidence outstanding, have him tell you how and where to attempt recovery.

● Before you conclude, review to make certain you have his unambiguous, unequivocal admissions to jurisdiction, elements of the corpus, ID and facts negating any legal defense. Then ask if there's anything else he wants to tell you — he may have been saving something back that never occurred to you to ask about.

● After you conclude the interrogation, stay with your strategy. Some of what the suspect has told you may not check out and you might need to conduct further interrogation. Keep your options open.

● Practice. Depending on your assignment, you may not have frequent opportunities for actual interrogation sessions, although you're expected to come through whenever necessary. If you make it a habit to interrogate every suspect you arrest — regardless of the offense — not only will you be consistently presenting better cases to the prosecutor, but you'll also be practicing for that make-or-break interrogation in a major case that will fall in your lap unexpectedly someday.

You can also refine your decoy questioning techniques through practice in the course of routine ped checks and auto stops. Practice will help you learn to control you subject's alertness level through voice, expression and demeanor, and will improve your ability to detect attempted deception. Reading this book will give you the *information*, but only practice will give you the *feel* for successful interrogation. Practice.

## Chapter 14

# PROOF TECHNIQUES

Getting the confession is only helpful if you can *prove* you got it. Proof requirements are dictated by the nature of the evidentiary problems typically encountered in pretrial motions and at trial.

Although the suspect may talk willingly to you in a one-on-one, informal setting, you can bet your badge he's not going to get up in court and embrace the confession you took, if he has any other way to go. As soon as he gets an attorney, the search will be on for ways to wiggle out of his statements. The defense attorney's checklist for spotting loopholes, then, is *your* checklist for closing them. He will be checking the following:

1) What proof is there to show whether or not the suspect had been legally detained or arrested at the time of interrogation? Is there a valid argument that the confession was the fruit of the poisonous tree?

2)    If no *Miranda* warning and waiver occurred, what proof is there as to whether or not the suspect was "in custody" when his statements were taken?

3)    If no *Miranda*, what proof is there as to whether or not the suspect's statements were the product of "interrogation,"or its functional equivalent?

4)    If a *Miranda* warning was given, how can the prosecution prove that it was adequate?

5)    How will the prosecution prove the suspect understood his rights?

6)    Is there any evidence that the suspect was "threatened, tricked or cajoled" into a waiver?

7)    How can the prosecution prove that the suspect intelligently waived his rights per *Miranda*?

8)    Had the suspect's right to counsel under the Sixth Amendment attached before interrogation? If so, what proof is there that the suspect personally reinitiated discussions and validly waived counsel?

9)    Prior to confessing, did the suspect say or do anything which could be construed as an invocation of his *Miranda* rights? If so, what proof is there that the police "scrupulously honored" his invocation? That the suspect personally reinitiated and waived?

10)    What evidence is there tending to show the suspect lacked the "rational intellect" to give a voluntary

statement? How will the prosecution prove his mental capacity?

11) Is there any evidence of unlawful force, threats, intimidation, or express or implied promises of leniency which might make the confession involuntary under the Fourteenth Amendment?

12) What proof is there that both the interrogator and the suspect were discussing one and the same crime when the suspect confessed? How did the police tie the suspect to this particular offense during interrogation?

13) Did the confession fail to establish jurisdictional elements of time and place, and if so, does the prosecution have any other means of proof?

14) Did the suspect admit to each and every element of the corpus, including any special knowledge, motive or intent or other mental condition required to prove the crime? If not, how will the prosecution prove these?

15) Did the suspect admit that he himself committed the crime? If so, did he describe which acts he personally performed and what each accomplice did?

16) What legal defenses are there to the crimes the suspect is charged with? What information is there to support or negate each such defense?

17) Can the police prove the content of the suspect's confession by tape recording or writing? If not, how

well-documented are details in the report? How much
information will be forgotten by the date of trial? Will
the prosecution be left with a one-to-one credibility
contest between the officer's recollections and the
suspect's?

18) If the suspect signed a written confession, is it something he wrote himself, or was it written or typed by
the police? Can the suspect argue that he just signed
what the police put in front of him? Is there proof he
reads and writes English? Is the written document
filled with police language, legal terms and vocabulary which is obviously unfamiliar to the suspect?

19) If the interrogation was taped, is it audible? Is it clear
who is speaking? Are there any "missing gaps" to
permit the suspect to claim promises or coercion took
place off the tape? How can the prosecution prove this
is the tape they say it is?

Get the idea? You don't have to give the defense
lawyer a very big loophole — he'll be grateful for
small favors. And he'll make the most of them, at your
expcnsc. A fcw additional proof considerations:

20) If a taped or written confession isn't feasible, try to
have a concealed witness to the oral cop-out for
corroboration. Standard jury instructions tell the ju-
rors they should "view any evidence of an oral confession with caution." And they do. Try not to force the
jury into deciding whether to believe *your* testimony
that the defendant confessed or *his* denial.

21)     Once the suspect has committed to his statement during an untaped interrogation, go back through the details, taking complete notes which *capture the suspect's own words, verbatim.*

22)     In your police report, do not state simply that "the suspect admitted to the crime." In two years, when the case comes up for trial, will you be able to recall *his* words? If not, you don't have a cop-out, because your conclusionary language is legally inadmissible. Don't draw conclusions — report the suspect's *exact words* as to understanding his rights ("Yeah, I do"), waiving his rights ("OK, I don't mind talking"), and every necessary admission ("I did it because he was an asshole, man...why the fuck do you think I did it?").

23)     When two or more suspects cop out, don't report that "they admitted their involvement in the crime." That kind of statement is inadmissible in court against either of them. Marry each suspect to his own words.

24)     Have the suspect demonstrate his reading, writing and comprehension levels by asking him to write something out in his own words — either his confession, or his understanding of his rights, or how he feels about what happened. Preserve this evidence to prevent the defense of "My English not too good. Not understanding."

25)     If you can't tape (best) but you can get the statement in writing (next best), let the suspect write it himself, after he's given you a confirmed oral commitment. Don't dictate what you want him to write ("They told

me what to write and I wrote it that way, Your Honor, but that's not what really happened"). After you check over his written narrative and see all the points he hasn't covered, write out a list of questions, leaving space for him to answer, and let him write in his won responses. Continue this process until you have him unambiguously and unequivocally committed in writing to every essential fact. Be patient. Be thorough.

26)    Have the suspect sign and date his confession, and then have a witness sign it.

27)    If you're able to tape (always try to in your more serious cases), be sure equipment is working, batteries are new, blank tapes are new and clearly labeled with case number and date, and microphones are picking up both you and the suspect clearly. Eliminate background noise. Record the serial number of your tape machines.

28)    Consider *double* taping, especially in homicide and high-publicity cases. If you use two machines, you guard against problems caused by equipment failure, and by *staggering* the "changeover" times, you'll be sure to have one tape rolling at all times. This prevents the suspect claiming later — as they almost always seem to do — that while you were turning the tape cassette over, you had an improper "off the record" discussion which tainted the remainder of the statement. Also, double taping on a staggered basis prevents the awful situation in which the suspect is on the verge of breaking, the tape runs out, and by the time

*Never interrupt a suspect in the midst of a spontaneous statement. Volunteered statements are not subject to Miranda, since no interrogation is involved.*

you get it ready again, he's changed his mind and you lose him.

29) Tapes need "signatures," for technical reasons. Allow a little bit of "leader" to run at the beginning of each side before you start talking.

30) Don't interrupt or talk over the suspect on the tape. *His* answers are what's important, not *your* magnificent voice. Let him be heard, unless he's rambling completely out of control and you need to redirect him.

31) Because suspects sometimes want to tell you something without the tape running, it's good to have your concealed corroboration witness even though you're taping, so you can prove what was — and wasn't — said and done off tape.

32) Make extra copies of taped and written confessions, to have in case of accidental loss or erasure. clearly label "original" and "copy." Keep your handwritten notes. Preserve proof of the confession until the prosecutor authorizes its destruction, or it's entered into evidence.

33) In your reports to the prosecutor, be sure to disclose all of the information you have relating to the suspect's waivers, admissions, confessions, and denials. Don't guess about their admissibility or importance — let the prosecutor decide these matters on the basis of complete details.

34) As always, review the evidence before taking the witness stand on a motion to exclude the statements, or

at the trial itself. *Know* what you did and did not do and say in your contacts with the suspect. *Know* what he did and did not tell you — in his words. Don't depend on your memory or a summary report several weeks or months after the interrogation. Be prepared to be accurate and precise in court.

What you're going to find, if you haven't already, is that as your skill as an interrogator and your attention to proof requirements improve, the frequency of your having to go to court will decline. Unless it's a do-or-die case, neither the defendant nor his lawyer is going to waste time and effort putting on a trial in a case where the evidence offers them no hope of escaping justice.

Any experienced defense attorney knows all too well the truth of Justice White's pronouncement about a defendant's own confession being the most damaging evidence possible. A case with a complete and admissible confession is the very *last* kind of case the defense attorney wants to have to try. That's why you don't often see skillful interrogators going to court. Their cases are more likely to be concluded at an early stage, by a plea of guilty.

As a law enforcement officer, that's the place you want to get to. You want to be so smooth, so good and so thorough at producing legally admissible waivers and confessions that you leave the crook no place to go but to jail. When you reach that point, you're practicing what for hundreds of years has been regarded as the ultimate skill in the criminal investigation profession — the art of interrogation.

> Confessions remain a proper element in law enforcement.
>
> *Miranda v. Arizona*

# POST SCRIPT

I probably don't have to tell you that the area of admissibility of confessions is, along with search and seizure, one of the two least-understood and most-changing fields in all of criminal law. Every succeeding US Supreme Court decision on confessions adds some new refinement.

I strongly recommend that you follow a plan for keeping current on the implications of 4th, 5th, 6th and 14th Amendment decisions for your interrogation activity. To do this, you may want to subscribe to and read one or more of the law enforcement publications available (check with your training officer), take a refresher course periodically, and stay in consultation with your local supervisors, legal advisor, training personnel, police science educators and prosecuting attorneys for information on significant developments.

Once you digest the law and master the art of interrogation, don't let yourself get out of date or out of practice. And don't forget to share what you learn with others. We're all students and we're all teachers.

**Good luck!**

# TABLE OF CASES

## US CASES CITED

## CALIFORNIA CASES CITED